DO Drops

Volume 13

DO Drops

Volume 13

Daily Bible Devotional

Dr. Bo Wagner

Word of His Mouth Publishers
Mooresboro, NC

All Scripture quotations are taken from the **King James Version** of the Bible.

ISBN: 978-1-941039-58-8
Printed in the United States of America
©2025 Dr. Bo Wagner

Word of His Mouth Publishers
Mooresboro, NC
www.wordofhismouth.com

Cover art by Chip Nuhrah

Devotion 01

As chapter thirty-one begins, there is an almost whiplash-like segue in subject. It is clear that Job knew his friends/attackers had not been swayed and still believed him to be a most wretched and wicked man, so Job will address that subject once again.

Job 31:1 *I made a covenant with mine eyes; why then should I think upon a maid?* **2** *For what portion of God is there from above? and what inheritance of the Almighty from on high?*

The unstated accusation that Job is defending himself against in verse one is that of lust. He clearly believed that his friends viewed him as one with an insatiable eye for looking at women in a lustful way. But it is in Job's assertion otherwise that we find an incredibly valuable bit of instruction. We would think that Job would have said, "I made a covenant with mine eyes; why then should I LOOK upon a maid?" but instead, he says, "*I made a covenant with mine eyes; why then should I THINK upon a maid?*" In other words, Job knew that if he thought it in his mind, he would likely act on it in his life. He knew that wherever he allowed his thoughts to settle and dwell, his doings would follow. And he knew that if he thought wrong and then acted wrong, he would be robbing himself of the blessings of God.

That is something that every one of us needs to remember every moment of every day!

Don't just determine to do right; that will never be enough. DO determine to always THINK right, and the doing will spring out of that!

Personal Notes:

_____

_____

_____

_____

_____

_____

_____

_____

_____

_____

_____

_____

_____

_____

_____

_____

_____

_____

_____

_____

_____

_____

_____

_____

Devotion 02

In verses one and two, Job again defended himself against the accusation of lust. But it was not just general lust that Job knew his friends suspected him of; it extended to actual adultery. So, Job now goes on to deal with that specific sin of which he was not at all subtly suspected.

Job 31:7 *If my step hath turned out of the way, and mine heart walked after mine eyes, and if any blot hath cleaved to mine hands;* **8** *Then let me sow, and let another eat; yea, let my offspring be rooted out.* **9** *If mine heart have been deceived by a woman, or if I have laid wait at my neighbour's door;* **10** *Then let my wife grind unto another, and let others bow down upon her.* **11** *For this is an heinous crime; yea, it is an iniquity to be punished by the judges.* **12** *For it is a fire that consumeth to destruction, and would root out all mine increase.*

When Job spoke in verse nine about the suspicion that his heart had been deceived by a woman and he had laid wait at his neighbor's door, it is the picture of one who waits until his neighbor is gone and then commits adultery with the man's wife. This very thought was so heinous to Job that in verse ten, he basically said, "If I have done this with another woman, and to her husband, then let the exact same thing be done with my wife by someone else." That is a pretty severe thing to say! Naturally, Job was not worried about this since he had not committed adultery. But it is his description of that particular sin in verses eleven and twelve that is so instructive. He called it a heinous crime, an iniquity to be punished by the judges, and a fire that consumes all increase. Job viewed adultery as one of the most filthy, degrading, abominable sins in the sight of God.

And all the rest of Scripture bears him out on that. Years later, Solomon especially would describe it in much the same terms in the book of Proverbs.

And yet today, society takes this sin very lightly. It is the subject of sitcoms and movies, and even most churches do not bat an eye at it. But God has never changed His view on this horrible sin. If you commit adultery, you have gone pretty much as low as you can go in the sight of God.

DO stay a virgin until marriage, DO be one hundred percent faithful to your spouse, and DO NOT ever commit adultery!

Personal Notes:

_____

_____

_____

_____

_____

_____

_____

_____

_____

Devotion 03

As Job continued his closing argument, he took a moment to discuss a very relevant present-day issue for all of us.

Job 31:13 *If I did despise the cause of my manservant or of my maidservant, when they contended with me;* **14** *What then shall I do when God riseth up? and when he visiteth, what shall I answer him?* **15** *Did not he that made me in the womb make him? and did not one fashion us in the womb?*

In these verses, Job was asserting that he had treated the "less important people" in life as if they were just as important as everyone else. He spoke of his servants and told his attackers that he had not despised their cause when they contended with him about something. In other words, if they had a complaint, he took it seriously. He did so because of the realization that he was nothing but a servant to God, and he wanted God to treat him the same way! He understood that the same God who made and fashioned him in the womb did the exact same thing for all of those servants.

Several years ago, a missionary visited our church seeking support. As is often the case, it was maybe ten minutes before service, and I was in jeans and a T-shirt because I had just been fixing something. I was getting ready to run to the office and change when Mr. Missionary came in. I tried to greet him, but he immediately looked past me to an older gentleman in my church, impeccably dressed, with snow-white hair. He brusquely brushed me off without so much as telling me his name and rushed to that other gentleman. He thought he was the pastor...

That did not work out so well for him.

DO remember that your character is demonstrated not by how you treat the "important" people in life but by whether or not you can treat everyone as if they are important, because they are! God made every one of us in His image; if you treat a waitress or busboy or trash collector poorly, you may as well be treating God Himself poorly.

Personal Notes:

_____
_____
_____
_____
_____
_____
_____
_____
_____
_____
_____
_____
_____
_____
_____
_____

Devotion 04

Job now deals with a very frequent accusation his attackers leveled against him, that he had not treated the poor well.

Job 31:17 O*r have eaten my morsel myself alone, and the fatherless hath not eaten thereof;* **18** *(For from my youth he was brought up with me, as with a father, and I have guided her from my mother's womb;)*

Mealtime among people in Bible lands in Biblical times was always supposed to be a time of hospitality, not just to friends but even to poor strangers. And Job's assertion was that in his house, that was indeed the case. He had always made the poor welcome and fed them at his table. But it is in verse eighteen that we find both very good guidance and also very vain hyperbole. Job said that he (the male orphan) was brought up with him and that Job had treated people like that as if he were their father. Then he said that she (the female orphan) had been guided by Job from his mother's womb, meaning from the day he was born.

Goo goo, ga, ga goo ga ga ga!

Job, my man...

Vain hyperbole aside, there is a great truth to learn here. We should not wait until our children are grown to teach them to be kind to those who are hurting and/or less fortunate. Even children are capable of being a help and blessing to others and should be taught to be just that.

DO teach your children early on to think of others!

Personal Notes:

_____

_____

_____

_____

_____

_____

_____

_____

_____

_____

_____

_____

_____

_____

_____

_____

_____

_____

_____

_____

_____

_____

_____

Devotion 05

As Job continues to defend himself, he turns to his previous behavior toward the needy. He then makes a really shocking request and an even more shocking motivation.

Job 31:19 *If I have seen any perish for want of clothing, or any poor without covering;* **20** *If his loins have not blessed me, and if he were not warmed with the fleece of my sheep;* **21** *If I have lifted up my hand against the fatherless, when I saw my help in the gate:* **22** *Then let mine arm fall from my shoulder blade, and mine arm be broken from the bone.* **23** *For destruction from God was a terror to me, and by reason of his highness I could not endure.*

Job had spent many years taking very good care of the poor, including feeding them and clothing them, and that with wool from his own sheep. Because of this, he had the confidence to say that if he had not done right concerning the less fortunate, *Then let mine arm fall from my shoulder blade, and mine arm be broken from the bone.*

I have never had "let my arm fall completely off" on my Bingo card of life, have you?

But the motivation for his behavior is what really gets to me. He said, *For destruction from God was a terror to me, and by reason of his highness I could not endure* [to do such wrong]. Job did right because he was terrified of God, and while the Bible certainly teaches the fear of the Lord, what Job was describing was something altogether different and darker. Living as if God is a horrible monster just looking for a reason to hurt us is a miserable existence! I am quite certain Job loved God as well; he makes that pretty clear throughout the book. But whatever time he spent in such needless terror of God was wasted time.

DO view God in the positive light that He deserves. Yes, He is holy, but He is also loving, forgiving, merciful, kind, and a thousand other things that ought to make us want to crawl up into His lap rather than cower in fear at the thought of Him!

Personal Notes:

_____

_____

_____

_____

_____

_____

_____

_____

_____

_____

_____

_____

_____

_____

_____

_____

_____

Devotion 06

In the next several verses, Job gives, ironically enough, some beautiful thoughts on sin. Mind you, sin is never beautiful, but the way that Job phrases this section truly is.

Job 31:24 *If I have made gold my hope, or have said to the fine gold, Thou art my confidence;* **25** *If I rejoiced because my wealth was great, and because mine hand had gotten much;* **26** *If I beheld the sun when it shined, or the moon walking in brightness;* **27** *And my heart hath been secretly enticed, or my mouth hath kissed my hand:* **28** *This also were an iniquity to be punished by the judge: for I should have denied the God that is above.*

In verses twenty-four through twenty-five, Job dealt with the self-confidence that very rich people often feel, a confidence that extends almost into arrogance and a belief that one has done it all in one's own power and wisdom. That, obviously, is easily understandable. But in verses twenty-six through twenty-eight, Job speaks of looking at the sun when it shines, or looking upward at the bright moon in the night sky, and his heart being enticed, and him kissing his hand.

What in the world is that about?

Short answer: It was called *Sabaeism*, meaning the worship of heavenly bodies. It was the idea that creation itself was divine rather than a product of the Divine. Job said, *This also were an iniquity to be punished by the judge: for I should have denied the God that is above.*

This ancient sin still very much exists today, only now we find it spoken in worshipful phrases like "mother earth" and "evolution" and in horoscopes and in all parts of the New Age movement and even in "The Church of Climate Change." It was idolatry then, and it is idolatry now. God called us to care for His creation, but never to worship it.

DO look at creation and wonder in awe. But DO so because of the God who created it!

Personal Notes:

_____

_____

_____

_____

_____

_____

_____

_____

_____

_____

_____

_____

_____

_____

_____

_____

_____

_____

Devotion 07

Job was nearing the end of his multi-chapter closing argument. And in the next several verses, he will speak in several generalities and one very eye-popping specific.

Job 31:29 *If I rejoiced at the destruction of him that hated me, or lifted up myself when evil found him:* **30** *Neither have I suffered my mouth to sin by wishing a curse to his soul.* **31** *If the men of my tabernacle said not, Oh that we had of his flesh! we cannot be satisfied.* **32** *The stranger did not lodge in the street: but I opened my doors to the traveller.* **33** *If I covered my transgressions as Adam, by hiding mine iniquity in my bosom:* **34** *Did I fear a great multitude, or did the contempt of families terrify me, that I kept silence, and went not out of the door?*

In verses twenty-nine and thirty, Job, in reference to his righteousness, told his friends that he had never even rejoiced when an enemy was struck down. In verse thirty-one, he pointed out that he fed everyone in his household with the best; he did not live on steak while expecting his servants to live on beans. In verse thirty-two, he pointed out that he consistently extended the customary hospitality of that day (since hotels were another four thousand or so years in coming) to any traveler, allowing him to come and sleep in his house rather than sleeping in the street.

But it is in verse thirty-three that we find a name, a specific and familiar name: Adam. Job said that he did not sin in the way that Adam sinned, by attempting to hide any of his iniquity. And, while there are unquestionably great spiritual truths that we can draw from that, what fascinates me the most is that Job, who seems to have lived in the years just after the flood of Genesis 6, regarded Adam as a literal, historical figure. This brilliant man, utterly familiar with the flood and Noah and all that preceded them, knew that Adam actually existed just as our Bible tells us. Job is one of the oldest books, if not the oldest book, in human history. And this ancient document confirms the historicity of the Genesis account.

DO believe your Bible just exactly as it is written!

Personal Notes:

_____

_____

_____

_____

_____

_____

_____

_____

_____

_____

_____

Devotion 08

Job will now unwittingly make one of the most ironic and unwise comments he has ever made.

Job 31:35 *Oh that one would hear me! behold, my desire is, that the Almighty would answer me, and that mine adversary had written a book.* **36** *Surely I would take it upon my shoulder, and bind it as a crown to me.*

Everything that Job said in these verses was a disaster. To begin with, someone did hear him; God heard every single word that he said. Secondly, he wished for God, whom he calls the Almighty, to answer him, having no clue how overmatched he will be when God does that very thing. Thirdly, he calls God his adversary when God had literally never been anything but good to him. Fourthly, though, Job comes to the subject of a book...

Job wished that God had written a book. And he said that if God ever did such a thing, he, Job, would put it upon his shoulder as if it were some kind of college honors sash and wear it as if it were a crown of glory. Little did Job know that God, at that very moment, was writing a book and that every detail of his story would be in it. He also had no clue about the nature of that book. He believed that if God ever did write a book, it would be a book with Job as the hero, utterly vindicated and thoroughly righteous, and with an apologetic God trying to make amends to him. And yet, that is not at all what God's book is like.

Everything about the Bible shows us our deficiencies and deep need for a Savior to rescue us from the sinful mess we humans have made of everything from the time of Adam forward. Job would not be the hero of God's book, nor are we the heroes of God's book. All of us, when we honestly look at Scripture, find ourselves as broken people desperately in need of rescue.

When you read this book that Job never got to read, DO recognize it for what it is. The Bible is God's story, and we are just in it!

Personal Notes:

_____

_____

_____

_____

_____

_____

_____

_____

_____

_____

_____

_____

_____

_____

_____

_____

_____

_____

Devotion 09

Job's jaw-dropping mistakes continue as he brings his argument to a close.

Job 31:37 *I would declare unto him the number of my steps; as a prince would I go near unto him.*

Job assured everyone who was listening that if he ever got to have a face-to-face meeting with God, he would declare unto God the number of his, Job's, steps, meaning that he would tell God exactly what his life had been like. He secondly claimed that if such a meeting ever took place, he would confidently stride right up to God as if he were a prince. And anyone who has ever read the book of Job knows that very shortly, Job will eat those words in the most dramatic fashion possible.

There is in mankind this individualistic pride that is constantly our undoing. Somehow, we believe that we are the ones constantly in the right, and we just cannot wait to get to heaven so that we can stride confidently up to the throne and God can say in everyone's hearing, "Yep, he/she was definitely right; all of you people should have listened!"

What utter folly. God knows your life better than you do. His evaluation of it was, "Their only hope is for me to come and die for them." So, DO take off any self-made, imaginary crown, "Prince" or "Princess," because the only thing good about you is Christ in you!

Personal Notes:

_____

_____

_____

_____

_____

_____

_____

_____

_____

_____

_____

_____

_____

_____

_____

_____

_____

_____

_____

_____

_____

_____

_____

_____

_____

Devotion 10

Here are the closing words of Job's argument to his friends/enemies.

Job 31:38 *If my land cry against me, or that the furrows likewise thereof complain;* **39** *If I have eaten the fruits thereof without money, or have caused the owners thereof to lose their life:* **40** *Let thistles grow instead of wheat, and cockle instead of barley. The words of Job are ended.*

In light of what Job said in the verses that immediately precede these, these words are actually very anticlimactic. Job moved from confidently asserting that if he could meet with God, he would stride up to Him as a prince to talking about the fact that he did right in all of his agricultural dealings. But it is his final words that are interesting to me:

The words of Job are ended.

By these words, Job very clearly meant, "I am done talking to you people about this matter." And for the rest of the book, he did not talk to them about that matter! He had a conversation with God, and we found that he later prayed for his friends, but Job never did reopen this argument.

Throughout this book, Job got many things right and many things wrong; file this one under "things he got right."

Have you ever been in an argument that made you want to start singing, "This is the fuss that never ends, it just goes on and on my friend, somebody

24

started fussing though we don't know who it was, and we'll just keep rehashing it forever just because, this is the fuss that never ends..."

What a waste of valuable time. DO learn the value of saying, "We're not going to agree, but we are going to stop fighting because I am hereby canceling my subscription to your issues!"

Personal Notes:

_____

_____

_____

_____

_____

_____

_____

_____

_____

_____

_____

_____

_____

_____

_____

_____

_____

_____

_____

_____

Devotion 11

At this point in the book of Job, things begin to change. The camera angle widens out for us, as it were, and shows us something that we were not made privy to before.

Job 32:1 *So these three men ceased to answer Job, because he was righteous in his own eyes.* **2a** *Then was kindled the wrath of Elihu the son of Barachel the Buzite, of the kindred of Ram...*

If you are reading these verses for the first time, your reaction is probably, "Wait, what? Who is this guy, and where did he come from?" And the answer, as we will see in the verses that follow, is that he had been there for the entire argument, quietly listening the whole time. In other words, there was an audience for the entire brouhaha. It is entirely probable that there was quite a sizable audience for it, in fact. Job's plight was so well known that Eliphaz, Zophar, and Bildad traveled a good way to get to Job. How much more likely is it that the locals were also gathered around?

And that provides us with a bit of an "aha!" moment, doesn't it? Throughout all the arguing back and forth, the speeches have been grandiose, self-glorifying, and repetitive. And that is exactly what you would expect with people who are playing to the crowd, trying to get them on their side.

In other words, this entire argument was doomed to failure from the outset. Nothing was going to be settled or accomplished because everyone wanted to be crowned the victor. Had Job's three friends pulled him aside quietly, apart from the crowd, and laid out their concerns, all of this likely would have gone down much more peacefully and successfully.

DO learn the value of keeping arguments from going public whenever possible. Once they do, it is only a matter of how badly everyone is going to lose, not a matter of who is going to win.

Personal Notes:

_____

_____

_____

_____

_____

_____

_____

_____

_____

_____

_____

_____

_____

_____

_____

_____

_____

_____

Devotion 12

From chapter thirty-two to chapter thirty-seven of Job, Elihu will be monologuing. But who is this man to begin with? Where in the world did he come from? Well, we are told in verse two that he was *the son of Barachel the Buzite, of the kindred of Ram.* Those names may not ring a bell with you, but one of their relatives' names will. Buz was the son of Nahor, brother of Abraham. Ram is the same as Aram, a nephew of Buz. In other words, Elihu was at least a great-great-nephew of Abraham. It is interesting to consider that Elihu, while merely a bystander, is the only person in the entire book of whom a detailed genealogy is given. So, Bible detectives, please put on your Sherlock Holmes hat, and see if you can come up with a logical reason why that is the case.

I'll wait...

Okay, time's up. Let's fast-forward a few verses and let Scripture itself give you a clue.

Job 32:15 *They were amazed, they answered no more: they left off speaking.* **16** *When I had waited, (for they spake not, but stood still, and answered no more;)* **17** *I said, I will answer also my part, I also will shew mine opinion.*

Elihu, in his monologue, started speaking to us, the readers! No one else in the entire book does that. The evidence suggests that Elihu is the author of the Book of Job, which is why we are given detailed information about him. This young man sat quietly for countless hours, letting the big boys do their thing. And then he wrote all of it down, and we are still getting help from it today. We do not know of one other thing that Elihu ever did in his entire life, but we do know that he helped to get part of the Bible into our hands today.

If all you ever do is get the Scripture into someone's hands, you have done something huge. Ninety-nine percent of Christians probably could not even tell you the name of this guy if you asked about him, but what he did has made an impact for God for four thousand years now.

In print, on social media, in every language on earth, DO get the Scripture to mankind!

Personal Notes:

_____

_____

_____

_____

_____

_____

_____

_____

_____

_____

_____

_____

_____

_____

Devotion 13

Now we know who Elihu was and that he was almost certainly the author of the Book of Job. However, we do not yet know his position on the issue at hand, namely the argument between Job and his three attackers. Here, then, is his position:

Job 32:2 *Then was kindled the wrath of Elihu the son of Barachel the Buzite, of the kindred of Ram: against Job was his wrath kindled, because he justified himself rather than God.* **3** *Also against his three friends was his wrath kindled, because they had found no answer, and yet had condemned Job.*

Elihu was angry at both sides. And that means that he took a third position entirely; one that has not yet been espoused by any human being in the book!

Job's position was that he was right, and therefore God was wrong. The attackers' position was that God was right, and therefore, Job was wrong. Elihu's position will be that God was right, and Job was right, but that Job was also wrong for making God out to be wrong, and the attackers were wrong for making Job out to be wrong. He especially hones in on the fact that they had no proof of their assertions against Job, yet continued to attack him anyway.

Elihu had an amazingly balanced, accurate assessment of the situation.

But how often do we find people dug into two opposing sides so fiercely that they fail to even consider the possibility of a third position? And how often are friendships ruined forever because of this?

When strife comes, DO consider that the two positions being argued may both be wrong to some degree, and DO be willing to hear from a wise voice that points out that possibility!

Personal Notes:

_____

_____

_____

_____

_____

_____

_____

_____

_____

_____

_____

_____

_____

_____

_____

_____

_____

_____

_____

_____

_____

_____

Devotion 14

Elihu will now begin to speak. And as he does, he begins by explaining why he waited so long to do so.

Job 32:4 *Now Elihu had waited till Job had spoken, because they were elder than he.* **5** *When Elihu saw that there was no answer in the mouth of these three men, then his wrath was kindled.* **6** *And Elihu the son of Barachel the Buzite answered and said, I am young, and ye are very old; wherefore I was afraid, and durst not shew you mine opinion.* **7** *I said, Days should speak, and multitude of years should teach wisdom.* **8** *But there is a spirit in man: and the inspiration of the Almighty giveth them understanding.*

Elihu had a pretty good understanding of proper manners. There was an issue being debated; the old men were having it out, so he, as a young man, waited his turn. That shows excellent manners and good methodology on his part. Had he interrupted while the old men were speaking, they would have taken pretty big umbrage with his behavior and likely would not have given him a fair hearing. That said, though, there did come a time for him to speak. And as he did so, he wisely did not try to put himself forth as if he were on their level; he did so on the basis of God giving him understanding.

"I'm just as smart as you" will never, ever go over well when dealing with someone older or more educated or more experienced than you. But, "Here is what God says," especially now that we can actually point to it in Scripture, will be acceptable to anyone who is truly saved and filled with the Holy Spirit.

DO learn your Bible well enough to be able to say, "Here is what God says!"

Personal Notes:

_____

_____

_____

_____

_____

_____

_____

_____

_____

_____

_____

_____

_____

_____

_____

_____

_____

_____

_____

_____

Devotion 15

As Elihu ramped up his speech to Job and his three attackers, here is what he said next.

Job 32:9 *Great men are not always wise: neither do the aged understand judgment.* **10** *Therefore I said, Hearken to me; I also will shew mine opinion.*

In verse nine, he stated what should be a universally acknowledged truth, which sadly isn't. Great men, meaning men who have achieved worldly success and acclaim, are not (always) wise. Old people do not (always) understand judgment, meaning the right way to look at things.

But then, in his next seemingly innocuous statement, he says something pretty important that often goes overlooked. He said, *I also will shew mine opinion*. The keyword there is "opinion." It is used exactly three times in the Book of Job. All three times are here in chapter thirty-two. All three times, it was used by Elihu.

Throughout the book, there were hundreds of opinions spouted by the two opposing sides. And yet neither of them regarded any of what they were saying as an opinion! No wonder they never made so much as an inch of progress in their "discussion."

The ability to recognize that our opinions are, in fact, OPINIONS, is a key skill in problem-solving.

So, unless you are dealing with a precept or principle of Scripture, DO learn to say the phrase, "in my opinion!"

Personal Notes:

_____

_____

_____

_____

_____

_____

_____

_____

_____

_____

_____

_____

_____

_____

_____

_____

_____

_____

_____

_____

_____

_____

_____

_____

Devotion 16

In verses eleven through fourteen, Elihu will speak directly to Eliphaz, Zophar, and Bildad. His speech will be simple where theirs were complicated, and unbiased where theirs were utterly one-sided.

Job 32:11 *Behold, I waited for your words; I gave ear to your reasons, whilst ye searched out what to say.* **12** *Yea, I attended unto you, and, behold, there was none of you that convinced Job, or that answered his words:* **13** *Lest ye should say, We have found out wisdom: God thrusteth him down, not man.* **14** *Now he hath not directed his words against me: neither will I answer him with your speeches.*

These verses confirm for us that Elihu was there from the beginning and heard it all. Elihu listened to all they had to say, and his correct estimation was, *"There was none of you that convinced Job, or that answered his words."* In other words, they said a lot, but absolutely nothing they said actually answered Job's assertions. They accused much; they proved nothing.

His last statement to them was, *"Now he hath not directed his words against me: neither will I answer him with your speeches."* In other words, the three attackers spoke much of what they spoke out of irritation. "How dare Job not simply agree to all of the horrible things we said about him! How dare he say we are wrong! The nerve!" But Job had not said a single word against Elihu, and therefore, he did not have an ax to grind in the debate. And that is something really essential for us to focus on. In any debate, if anything is going to be solved, one of two things must happen. People either need to acknowledge that they have an ax to grind, which then will help them try to avoid grinding it, or some truly neutral party must step in to arbitrate. Things rarely ever get solved by people who are blind to their own biases!

DO avoid ax-grinding, one way or the other!

Personal Notes:

_____

_____

_____

_____

_____

_____

_____

_____

_____

_____

_____

_____

_____

_____

_____

_____

_____

_____

Devotion 17

We now arrive at the point I alluded to just a few devotions ago, where Elihu clearly seems to reveal himself to be the author of the book:

Job 32:15 *They were amazed, they answered no more: they left off speaking.* **16** *When I had waited, (for they spake not, but stood still, and answered no more;)* **17** *I said, I will answer also my part, I also will shew mine opinion.*

Having done so, he will now describe what was going on inside him as he begins his speech:

Job 32:18 *For I am full of matter, the spirit within me constraineth me.* **19** *Behold, my belly is as wine which hath no vent; it is ready to burst like new bottles.*

If I may paraphrase, he said, "If I don't speak up, I'm gonna bust!"

And yet, he waited a very, very, very, very long time to speak. He waited until everyone had a turn, then another, then another, then another. And in a couple of cases, still another. So this young man, who was about to bust for wanting to speak, still had the composure to wait more than his turn to speak! And that may go a long way toward explaining why, when he was done, no one ever answered him back. A person who is exceedingly patient before they finally speak is not usually one who goes off half-cocked and says stupid things that can easily be refuted.

DO learn the value, not just of <u>thinking</u> before you speak, but of <u>waiting</u> before you speak!

Personal Notes:

_____

_____

_____

_____

_____

_____

_____

_____

_____

_____

_____

_____

_____

_____

_____

_____

_____

_____

_____

_____

_____

_____

_____

_____

_____

Devotion 18

All of chapter thirty-two is Elihu's introduction to his speech before he gets into the content. Here is how he ends that introduction:

Job 32:20 *I will speak, that I may be refreshed: I will open my lips and answer.* **21** *Let me not, I pray you, accept any man's person, neither let me give flattering titles unto man.* **22** *For I know not to give flattering titles; in so doing my maker would soon take me away.*

Those last two verses are an indication that Elihu is going to radically depart from what was going on in the debate up until that point. Job and his attackers had been engaged in a battle of stature: who was the "big dog" that everyone needed to ooh and ahh over? Elihu rightly regarded that as part of the problem. He said, "I am not going to give flattering titles to anyone here; if I did that, I believe God would kill me for it!" And while that may seem like a bit of melodrama, Elihu did not seem to think so at all. He regarded it as a very serious thing to engage in flattery while engaging in correction.

The principle is a good one. Whenever we have to arbitrate between parties, flattery is a sure sign that we cannot be trusted to be impartial and an indication that we do not understand that God is watching us, since He is the one who put us in that trusted position to begin with.

DO be impartial when called on to help settle differences; we would expect others to do the exact same thing for us!

Personal Notes:

_____

_____

_____

_____

_____

_____

_____

_____

_____

_____

_____

_____

_____

_____

_____

_____

_____

_____

_____

_____

_____

_____

_____

Devotion 19

As chapter thirty-three begins, Elihu is done speaking to the three attackers and turns his attention to Job. And his introduction was a good one, and one that Job, as indicated by his silence, seems to have appreciated:

Job 33:1 *Wherefore, Job, I pray thee, hear my speeches, and hearken to all my words.* **2** *Behold, now I have opened my mouth, my tongue hath spoken in my mouth.* **3** *My words shall be of the uprightness of my heart: and my lips shall utter knowledge clearly.*

This was Elihu's promise that he was not going to go beyond what he actually knew. Job's three attackers had made wild, horrible, unfounded assertions; Elihu determined to stick to a Detective Joe Friday "Just the facts, ma'am," kind of approach.

That had to be music to Job's ears after all the other three had put him through. Mind you, he was certainly not going to like everything that Elihu had to say, but at least he was not going to get called a widow-beater, arm-of-orphan breaker, thief, and all-around heartless monster.

This is such an important balance to strike. We will so often be called upon to say negative things to people. But what will make them much more willing to receive those negative statements is if we stick to the facts, nothing more and nothing less. So many times, when dealing with a spouse, or children, or co-worker, or friend, we make the mistake of "extrapolating." But as soon as we do, those we are trying to correct will seize on that extra, untrue material and shut down any discussion that could help with the real issue.

DO be more like Joe Friday than Chicken Little!

Personal Notes:

_____

_____

_____

_____

_____

_____

_____

_____

_____

_____

_____

_____

_____

_____

_____

_____

_____

_____

_____

_____

_____

_____

Devotion 20

As Elihu begins to address Job, he immediately does something that none of the other three ever bothered to do.

Job 33:4 *The Spirit of God hath made me, and the breath of the Almighty hath given me life. **5** If thou canst answer me, set thy words in order before me, stand up. **6** Behold, I am according to thy wish in God's stead: I also am formed out of the clay. **7** Behold, my terror shall not make thee afraid, neither shall my hand be heavy upon thee.*

Throughout the book, Job had loudly wished for a chance to present his argument and make his defense to God. Elihu simply offered to stand in for God on that one! In so many words, he said, "You could not handle speaking to God; you would be terrified. So speak to me and say whatever it is you want to say to God. I am a man, like you, so you will not be afraid, but I am also made by God, so I will make a good substitute in this instance. The others have not listened, but I will if you still want to speak at any point."

How many times do you just wish you could stand before God and complain, knowing good and well that if you ever did stand before God, all you would do is bow! But since that is the case, it is pretty helpful to have a human, made by God, to stand in and let us vent. Sometimes you just need to tell your side of the story!

DO be willing to be a listening ear; that may be all that it takes to keep someone from losing hope!

Personal Notes:

_____

_____

_____

_____

_____

_____

_____

_____

_____

_____

_____

_____

_____

_____

_____

_____

_____

_____

_____

_____

_____

_____

_____

_____

Devotion 21

Elihu is now going to do something that truly is new ground in the book and in the argument.

Job 33:8 *Surely thou hast spoken in mine hearing, and I have heard the voice of thy words, saying,* **9** *I am clean without transgression, I am innocent; neither is there iniquity in me.* **10** *Behold, he findeth occasions against me, he counteth me for his enemy,* **11** *He putteth my feet in the stocks, he marketh all my paths.* **12** *Behold, in this thou art not just: I will answer thee, that God is greater than man.*

I told you several devotions ago that Job's position was that he was right, and therefore God was wrong. The attackers' position was that God was right, and therefore Job was wrong. Elihu's position was that God was right, and Job was right, but that Job was also wrong for making God out to be wrong. And now we see that clearly. Unlike the accusers, Elihu did not charge Job with previous crimes and wrongs; he merely told Job that he was wrong for accusing God of doing wrong. That was absolutely a new approach and the right approach.

Elihu went on to make a very simple yet powerful statement, one that God Himself quickly echoed once he spoke up: God is greater than man. In other words, sometimes (a lot of times, actually), we are just going to have to trust Him. He really does not owe us any answers or any information. He often gives both of those things out of His kindness and grace, but He owes us nothing.

On the days when you have done right and yet feel like God is wrong because you have been wronged, DO remember that God is never wrong, and implying that He is makes us wrong!

Personal Notes:

_____
_____
_____
_____
_____
_____
_____
_____
_____
_____
_____
_____
_____
_____
_____
_____
_____
_____
_____
_____
_____
_____

Devotion 22

As Elihu continues speaking to Job, his focus remains solidly on the sovereignty of God.

Job 33:13 *Why dost thou strive against him? for he giveth not account of any of his matters.* **14** *For God speaketh once, yea twice, yet man perceiveth it not.* **15** *In a dream, in a vision of the night, when deep sleep falleth upon men, in slumberings upon the bed;* **16** *Then he openeth the ears of men, and sealeth their instruction,* **17** *That he may withdraw man from his purpose, and hide pride from man.* **18** *He keepeth back his soul from the pit, and his life from perishing by the sword.*

Elihu's opening question and answer show a good understanding of the power and nature of God. Striving against Him is nothing but wasted effort because He does not and will not answer to man. The Creator owes the creation exactly nothing by way of explanation on anything. That said, though, verses fifteen through eighteen show the graciousness of God in often giving us tidbits of guidance on a personal level. Elihu mentioned dreams, which in the days before Scripture were one of God's primary ways of speaking to man. He gave those dreams, as Elihu reminded Job, to pull men back from any prideful purposes and, in so doing, preserve their lives.

So, we see that the God who owes us no information and resists any demands on our part often graciously gives us what we do not deserve, just because He is good and He loves us. It is almost like He is the King of kings, and we are His subjects.

If you want to avoid being perpetually frustrated, DO remember that He is not just baby Jesus, He is KING Jesus!

Personal Notes:

_____
_____
_____
_____
_____
_____
_____
_____
_____
_____
_____
_____
_____
_____
_____
_____
_____
_____
_____
_____
_____

Devotion 23

As Elihu continues, he uses a word that has only been used once in the book thus far: the word chasten.

Job 33:19 *He is chastened also with pain upon his bed, and the multitude of his bones with strong pain:*

Here is the other time it was used:

Job 5:17 *Behold, happy is the man whom God correcteth: therefore despise not thou the chastening of the Almighty:*

In Job 5:17, Eliphaz used the word chastening to begin to try to prove to Job that he had been horribly wicked. Now Elihu is using it again. So, is Elihu about to go the same route and take the same position as Job's three attackers? Thankfully, the answer is no, or at least not yet. Elihu is still speaking about how God communicates with His children. He just finished mentioning dreams, and now he mentions chastening. Elihu is taking the same position that the writer of Hebrews would take thousands of years later:

Hebrews 12:6 *For whom the Lord loveth he chasteneth, and scourgeth every son whom he receiveth.*

For the next few verses, Elihu goes on to show the benefits of chastisement. And yet, at no time does he accuse Job of stealing from widows or breaking the arms of orphaned children. In other words, he gives

Job a new way to view his trials. Job had viewed them as a sign that God was indifferent to him, even though he was righteous; his attackers viewed them as a sign that God hated him because he was evil; Elihu posits that God loves him and wants to make him even better through his sufferings!

When hard times come, and there seems to be no sin, no stupidity, no reason why, DO consider that God in love may just be making you even better, more like Him!

Personal Notes:

_____

_____

_____

_____

_____

_____

_____

_____

_____

_____

_____

_____

_____

_____

_____

_____

_____

_____

Devotion 24

Elihu has spoken to Job thus far about dreams being used by God to instruct man and chastening being used by God to instruct man. Now he will bring forth another tool that God uses to instruct those whom He loves.

Job 33:23 *If there be a messenger with him, an interpreter, one among a thousand, to shew unto man his uprightness:* **24** *Then he is gracious unto him, and saith, Deliver him from going down to the pit: I have found a ransom.*

Elihu was pointing out that God often uses a very wise messenger to instruct the one He loves and wishes to improve. Such a man was a "one out of a thousand" kind of person. Note the subtle jab at Job's attackers in this; not three of a thousand, but one of a thousand.

Elihu was humbly pointing to himself in this. Who knows who sent the three hateful attackers, maybe the devil, maybe they just chose to come. But when God sends a man by who can "interpret" what is going on and show man the way of uprightness within whatever he is going through, and when that man responds appropriately, God often changes everything. The way Elihu put it here was that God would be gracious and say, *Deliver him from going down to the pit: I have found a ransom.* In other words, I have found something in him that makes Me want to change things for him.

And all of that would start with a man being willing to speak the truth in an uncomfortable situation, and the person to whom he is speaking responding appropriately.

DO thank God for people who speak God's wisdom to you, even if you do not want to hear it. It is usually the beginning of a big change for the better when you do!

Personal Notes:

_____

_____

_____

_____

_____

_____

_____

_____

_____

_____

_____

_____

_____

_____

_____

_____

_____

_____

Devotion 25

After having spoken to Job about the fact that God would often send a wise man to a person so that person could hear instruction and be improved, Elihu will now give Job some pretty specific hope that would come from that.

Job 33:25 *His flesh shall be fresher than a child's: he shall return to the days of his youth:* **26** *He shall pray unto God, and he will be favourable unto him: and he shall see his face with joy: for he will render unto man his righteousness.* **27** *He looketh upon men, and if any say, I have sinned, and perverted that which was right, and it profited me not;* **28** *He will deliver his soul from going into the pit, and his life shall see the light.*

Sitting there with skin thickened and mangled like an elephant hide, Job had to react to the words, *His flesh shall be fresher than a child's: he shall return to the days of his youth.* Elihu's belief concerning this was that God *looketh upon men, and if any say, I have sinned, and perverted that which was right, and it profited me not; He will deliver his soul from going into the pit, and his life shall see the light.*

Now, think on this. Job's attackers had accused him of sin, and he reacted angrily against it. But here is Elihu accusing him of sin, and he says nothing. What is the difference? Again, the difference is that Elihu only accused him of what was true and accurate: speaking against God. The others made things up, and the viler, the better.

If you are going to point out sin in people's lives, DO make sure you only point at what is actually there, not at all of the things that aren't!

Personal Notes:

_____

_____

_____

_____

_____

_____

_____

_____

_____

_____

_____

_____

_____

_____

_____

_____

_____

_____

_____

_____

_____

_____

_____

Devotion 26

For all of the wise things that Elihu has said thus far, a single word he will say in the next couple of verses is, to me, one of the wisest, a word that gives me hope that people can indeed be accurate and level-headed.

Job 33:29 *Lo, all these things worketh God oftentimes with man,* **30** *To bring back his soul from the pit, to be enlightened with the light of the living.*

Oftentimes. It seems like a filler word, but that is not remotely the case. This is the first time the word occurs in the entire Bible, and it makes me want to shout, "Finally! Somebody gets it!"

This word, applied to God by Elihu, is an acknowledgment that though God usually does a particular thing a particular way, He is not bound to always do it that way. Throughout their attacks, Job's trio of taunters continually said, in so many words, "God always does things the exact same way, and we know what that way is, so you are doubtless horribly wicked." And no protests by Job, no assurances that he had not harmed orphans or robbed widows, could ever change their minds. Had they ever stopped to consider that maybe God was capable of a great deal of variety in His dealings and that they, as creatures, could not possibly know everything there was to know about the Creator, they may have approached the subject with a great deal more humility.

DO practice this statement very regularly: "Nice box you have there; just don't expect God to jump into it for you!"

Personal Notes:

_____

_____

_____

_____

_____

_____

_____

_____

_____

_____

_____

_____

_____

_____

_____

_____

_____

_____

_____

_____

_____

_____

_____

_____

_____

Devotion 27

Elihu was on a roll and took the last few verses of chapter thirty-three to address Job directly.

Job 33:31 *Mark well, O Job, hearken unto me: hold thy peace, and I will speak.* **32** *If thou hast any thing to say, answer me: speak, for I desire to justify thee.* **33** *If not, hearken unto me: hold thy peace, and I shall teach thee wisdom.*

Elihu both encouraged Job to quietly listen to him and also offered to let him speak if he desired to do so. That is a refreshing change from the belligerence of Job's attackers. But it is what Elihu said at the end of verse thirty-two that probably made Job cry tears of gratitude, *I desire to justify thee.*

Let those words sink in. For hour after hour after hour, Job fought a three-against-one battle against people who desperately wanted to condemn him. Now he was being instructed by a young man who had the exact opposite goal: he wanted to justify him. He wanted to find a way to clear his name. He did not want to find out that Job had been horrible; he wanted to find out that Job had actually been righteous and had just responded wrong because he did not understand.

Elihu was giving Job something more precious than gold: the benefit of the doubt.

If we ever find ourselves actually wanting to find out that people have done horrible things, there is something desperately wrong with us. DO seek the truth, but DO actually hope you are wrong about any bad things you suspect of others!

Personal Notes:

_____

_____

_____

_____

_____

_____

_____

_____

_____

_____

_____

_____

_____

_____

_____

_____

_____

_____

_____

_____

_____

_____

_____

_____

_____

_____

Devotion 28

As chapter thirty-four begins, Elihu once again addresses all four of the men before him, Job, Eliphaz, Bildad, and Zophar.

Job 34:1 *Furthermore Elihu answered and said,* **2** *Hear my words, O ye wise men; and give ear unto me, ye that have knowledge.* **3** *For the ear trieth words, as the mouth tasteth meat.* **4** *Let us choose to us judgment: let us know among ourselves what is good.*

As in so many other things, this marks a departure from what took place in the entire argument between Job and his attackers. They spent their time proclaiming themselves wise and the opposition as foolish, or at least not as wise as they were. Elihu takes the approach of acknowledging that they were all men of knowledge and wisdom. So right off the bat, he gains their willingness to listen to him. From there, he proposes a solution to the argument, namely that they all listen carefully and evaluate all of the words spoken, then discern proper judgment of the situation from there. And he uses the word "us" three times in that proposal.

If you get the sense that this version of Elihu would probably make a really good statesman, I suspect you are correct.

When we deal with others with whom we have disagreements, our best starting point, if possible, is "How can we, together, work our way through this and come to a meeting of the minds?" Mind you, the other side may prove to be so ornery as to not be in the least bit interested in that offer, but people of good will and reasonable mind generally will.

DO aim to be more of a spiritual statesman than a spiritual prosecuting attorney!

Personal Notes:

_____

_____

_____

_____

_____

_____

_____

_____

_____

_____

_____

_____

_____

_____

_____

_____

_____

_____

_____

_____

_____

_____

_____

Devotion 29

Elihu will now begin to deal specifically with Job's error. And if you pay attention, you will once again find that it is all about the present, not about the past.

Job 34:5 *For Job hath said, I am righteous: and God hath taken away my judgment.* **6** *Should I lie against my right? my wound is incurable without transgression.* **7** *What man is like Job, who drinketh up scorning like water?* **8** *Which goeth in company with the workers of iniquity, and walketh with wicked men.* **9** *For he hath said, It profiteth a man nothing that he should delight himself with God.*

Notice how Elihu starts and ends this segment; he does so with the phrases, *Job hath said*, and *For he hath said*. Elihu is carefully maintaining his original position that it is not anything that Job previously did that makes him wrong; it is what he has now said that makes him wrong. Elihu accurately paraphrases the entire argument of Job by saying, *I am righteous: and God hath taken away my judgment. Should I lie against my right? my wound is incurable without transgression.*

That was indeed Job's position. Simply put, he knew he had done nothing wrong, but he then swerved into the error of thinking that God had, and he said so. Elihu then concludes, *What man is like Job, who drinketh up scorning like water? Which goeth in company with the workers of iniquity, and walketh with wicked men.* All of that means, "Job has gotten to be a professional at scorning; he drinks it up like it is water. And in so doing, he has unwittingly joined in with the wicked who also accuse God of wrongdoing."

Elihu was correct. Mind you, he himself may not have done any better in Job's place, but he was still correct. No matter what we go through and how righteously we have lived, no matter how badly those two things seem to not match, God never does wrong.

DO remember that God never does wrong, and DO make sure your lips never accuse Him of doing so!

Personal Notes:

_____
_____
_____
_____
_____
_____
_____
_____
_____
_____
_____
_____
_____
_____
_____

Devotion 30

Elihu, as he already pointed out, wanted to justify Job. But whether he could do that or not, he knew that he could, and therefore would, justify God. The next few verses provide an excellent example of him doing so.

Job 34:10 *Therefore hearken unto me, ye men of understanding: far be it from God, that he should do wickedness; and from the Almighty, that he should commit iniquity.* **11** *For the work of a man shall he render unto him, and cause every man to find according to his ways.* **12** *Yea, surely God will not do wickedly, neither will the Almighty pervert judgment.*

Once again, showing respect to all four of the men he was disagreeing with, Elihu addresses them all as *men of understanding*. He then tells those men of understanding that God will never commit iniquity. Whether they knew it or not, Job's three adversaries were as guilty as Job in this; God had proclaimed Job as perfect and upright, and they proclaimed Job to be vile and filthy, thereby unknowingly accusing God of lying. But God will never do wrong either by lying or by treating someone unjustly. Elihu observed in verse eleven that God would always treat men according to their works, good or bad.

But where did that leave Job? He did right and yet suffered horribly. But remember, that was Satan's doing, not God's! God did, in fact, always bless Job for Job's uprightness, and we see that specifically in his great blessings at the beginning and at the end of the book. Elihu was exactly right when he said, *surely God will not do wickedly, neither will the Almighty pervert judgment.*

When you cannot seem to figure out where something is coming from, DO remember this formula: if it has God's fingerprints on it, it isn't the devil, and if it has the devil's fingerprints on it, it isn't God!

Personal Notes:

_____
_____
_____
_____
_____
_____
_____
_____
_____
_____
_____
_____
_____
_____
_____
_____
_____
_____
_____
_____

Devotion 31

Although Genesis was not yet written, in the next few verses, Elihu will show a good understanding of what took place at the creation and what impact it has on man even in our day.

Job 34:13 *Who hath given him a charge over the earth? or who hath disposed the whole world?* **14** *If he set his heart upon man, if he gather unto himself his spirit and his breath;* **15** *All flesh shall perish together, and man shall turn again unto dust.*

The answer to Elihu's questions in verse thirteen is "no one." God is the Creator of all and, therefore, in authority over all. No one had to give Him that; it has always been His. But it is in verses thirteen and fourteen that we find the impact of that truth. When Elihu said, *if he* [God] *set his heart upon man*, it means to really focus on man in anger. Both Job and his adversaries had inferred that God does that very thing. But Elihu went on to say, *if he gather unto himself his spirit and his breath; All flesh shall perish together, and man shall turn again unto dust.*

When God formed man, He breathed into his nostrils the breath of life (Genesis 2:7). That breath has passed from person to person down through the millennia.

Do something, please. Take a good, deep breath...

Did you enjoy that? I hope so, because that breath was God's breath, on loan to you. If God suddenly chose to take back His breath from mankind, we would all die together and go back to dust. So, since all four of those men were still breathing, God was still being kind to all of them!

But it kind of makes you think, doesn't it? Every time we breathe out either a kind or an unkind word, we are using God's breath to do it. Every time we breathe out either a pure or a filthy word, we are using God's breath to do it.

DO make sure that you use God's breath wisely, so He is inclined to keep on letting you use it!

Personal Notes:

_____

_____

_____

_____

_____

_____

_____

_____

_____

_____

_____

_____

_____

_____

_____

_____

Devotion 32

As Elihu continues describing God and applying those descriptions to the situation at hand, he will now deal with a matter of hierarchy.

Job 34:16 *If now thou hast understanding, hear this: hearken to the voice of my words.* **17** *Shall even he that hateth right govern? and wilt thou condemn him that is most just?* **18** *Is it fit to say to a king, Thou art wicked? and to princes, Ye are ungodly?* **19** *How much less to him that accepteth not the persons of princes, nor regardeth the rich more than the poor? for they all are the work of his hands.*

Job, through his pain, had indeed accused God of despising that which was right. And yet, how could such a God govern a world in which there is so much injustice to be found? If God is all-powerful and yet hates that which is right, there would be no right at all, only constant wrong. This is an obvious point of logic that Job could no longer think clearly enough to see. And because Job could not see it, Elihu went on in verse nineteen to use a low earthly illustration of that high heavenly truth. One does not lightly accuse even an earthly king of wrongdoing since he is the final word in the kingdom! How much less, then, should anyone easily accuse God of wrongdoing when, according to verse nineteen, He never even plays favorites? Whether rich or poor, powerful or weak, God made all men and governs them with an even hand. That is the kind of King we serve!

Are those truths always obvious to us? No. There are times when it seems to us that God is indeed playing favorites and judging unjustly. But again, if He EVER did it, then He would ALWAYS do it! As the all-powerful God, He will either always be good or always be bad. And since we OFTEN see that He is good, we can thereby know that He is ALWAYS good.

We often say, "God is good." But for today, DO instruct yourself with these words, "God is always good!"

Personal Notes:

_____

_____

_____

_____

_____

_____

_____

_____

_____

_____

_____

_____

_____

_____

_____

_____

_____

Devotion 33

Continuing on in his verbal defense of God's character, Elihu will now come to a matter of indictment, which means "a formal accusation that a person has committed a crime."

Job 34:20 *In a moment shall they die, and the people shall be troubled at midnight, and pass away: and the mighty shall be taken away without hand.* **21** *For his eyes are upon the ways of man, and he seeth all his goings.* **22** *There is no darkness, nor shadow of death, where the workers of iniquity may hide themselves.* **23** *For he will not lay upon man more than right; that he should enter into judgment with God.*

The "they" of verse twenty refers back to both the rich and the poor in verse nineteen. Their wealth cannot save them, nor does their poverty make God overlook them. When it is time for them to die, they die whether anyone has laid a hand on them or not. And Elihu went on from there to observe that the wicked among them are not able to hide their doing from God, and therefore, God always gets it right when He judges them. But it is in verse twenty-three that Elihu brings out his main thought in these verses. God does know the difference between the righteous and the wicked, and He will never lay more judgment than He should upon any man. And here is the indictment: as the end of verse twenty-three points out, if God ever did lay upon man more than what was

70

just, man would have a legitimate reason to enter into judgment with God, meaning to get into a legal and moral debate with Him over the issue.

And God will never let that happen. And in Job's case, it certainly did not happen since it was the devil that brought every ounce of Job's pain, not God!

DO trust the God that never does you or anyone else wrong!

Personal Notes:

_____

_____

_____

_____

_____

_____

_____

_____

_____

_____

_____

_____

_____

_____

_____

_____

_____

_____

_____

_____

Devotion 34

As Elihu continues speaking to Job and vindicating God, he gives Job a very simple and direct instruction.

Job 34:31 *Surely it is meet to be said unto God, I have borne chastisement, I will not offend any more: **32** That which I see not teach thou me: if I have done iniquity, I will do no more.*

This instruction deals with what is and is not appropriate to say to God. Many times in our trials, we say some very inappropriate things to God. We do so because of what we do not know and what we assume. Therefore, the appropriate thing to say to God is, "For whatever reason, I seem to be under chastisement. Whatever I have done wrong, I won't do it anymore. Lord, please just show me what it is that I do not know. If I have done wrong, and you will show me, I will stop."

If. Why is that such an appropriate thing to say to God? Mostly because He knows all of the things that we do not know and loves us like no one else will ever love us!

If we keep those things in mind during our hard times, it will keep us from saying some things to God and about God that we later very much regret. Despite the fact that Job did right before his trial, during His trial, his complaints against God often crossed the line. He never went as far as the devil wanted him to go; he never cursed God. But he did very much bring God down to the level of being unjust in His dealings, and God is never unjust in his dealings.

God never has to use an "if" unless He wants to, but we are very wise to use the power of "if" when talking with Him about our trials. So DO use the power of "if" to harness your tongue against all of the harsh things you should never say!

Personal Notes:

_____
_____
_____
_____
_____
_____
_____
_____
_____
_____
_____
_____
_____
_____
_____
_____
_____
_____
_____
_____
_____

Devotion 35

Within the Book of Job, there is a very noticeable pattern. Job began just right, worshipping, and not charging God foolishly. But then, as time went on, he veered further and further into error. Job's three friends began just right, sitting quietly and comforting Job. But then, as time went on, they veered further and further into error. Sadly, the last guy up to bat, Elihu, will now make that exact same mistake. He began by speaking politely, and even telling Job that he desired to justify him. But now notice what he says:

Job 34:33 *Should it be according to thy mind? he will recompense it, whether thou refuse, or whether thou choose; and not I: therefore speak what thou knowest.* **34** *Let men of understanding tell me, and let a wise man hearken unto me.* **35** *Job hath spoken without knowledge, and his words were without wisdom.* **36** *My desire is that Job may be tried unto the end because of his answers for wicked men.* **37** *For he addeth rebellion unto his sin, he clappeth his hands among us, and multiplieth his words against God.*

In verse thirty-five, Elihu said, *Job hath spoken without knowledge, and his words were without wisdom.* That was entirely accurate and appropriate, and Job himself later admitted to that very thing. But Elihu then went into verse thirty-six and said, *My desire is that Job may be tried unto the end because of his answers for wicked men.* Yikes! Not even Eliphaz, Bildad, and Zophar wished that on Job. Elihu is calling for Job to be judged to the end, meaning to his utter demise.

And then, in verse thirty-seven, he said, *For he addeth rebellion unto his sin.* Um, excuse me, Elihu, but specifically what sin? Elihu blasted the three enemies of Job for accusing him without proof, and then turned right around and did the exact same thing! It's almost like it is a really bad idea just to keep talking and talking and talking...

And it is, especially when it comes to matters that only God knows the entirety of. If we really believe that God knows everything and will ultimately deal with everything, there is a lot of wisdom in just briefly speaking our minds and then letting things go before we end up saying something stupid.

DO know when to stop talking!

Personal Notes:

_____
_____
_____
_____
_____
_____
_____
_____
_____

Devotion 36

Elihu will have several ups and downs throughout the rest of his speech, and his next few phrases are still distinctly of the "down" variety.

Job 35:1 *Elihu spake moreover, and said,* **2** *Thinkest thou this to be right, that thou saidst, My righteousness is more than God's? 3 For thou saidst, What advantage will it be unto thee? and, What profit shall I have, if I be cleansed from my sin?*

Isn't it awful for Job to have said, "My righteousness is more than God's'? Well, it certainly would be, if he had ever actually said that! But if you begin again at the very first chapter of Job and read back up to this point, you will search for those words in vain, because Job never said them. So, why did Elihu make that accusation? Because, according to his reasoning in verse three, Job had said, *What advantage will it be unto thee? and, What profit shall I have, if I be cleansed from my sin?* If you are confused by how much of a stretch it seems to draw the one out of the other, you will doubtless be even more befuddled when you realize that when Job did say those words of verse three, he did so in Job 21:13-15 while pointing out what sinners say! It would be almost like you quoting the opening line of the Gettysburg Address and having your enemy say, "You said that America was born just eighty-seven years ago, so you must hate America and love communism!"

This is the kind of insanity you get when people are more concerned about proving their point than they are about arriving at the truth.

DO memorize a helpful phrase that should guide you in all of your debates and disagreements: Truth over Trophies!

Personal Notes:

_____

_____

_____

_____

_____

_____

_____

_____

_____

_____

_____

_____

_____

_____

_____

_____

_____

_____

_____

_____

_____

Devotion 37

Elihu will right the ship just a bit in the next few verses, making what should be some pretty obvious statements.

Job 35:4 *I will answer thee, and thy companions with thee.* **5** *Look unto the heavens, and see; and behold the clouds which are higher than thou.* **6** *If thou sinnest, what doest thou against him? or if thy transgressions be multiplied, what doest thou unto him?* **7** *If thou be righteous, what givest thou him? or what receiveth he of thine hand?* **8** *Thy wickedness may hurt a man as thou art; and thy righteousness may profit the son of man.*

In simple terms, it was Elihu's accurate assessment here that what we do really does not affect God. We neither make God dirtier or smaller by our sin, nor do we make God purer or bigger by our righteousness. What we do affects people, but not God. And that one simple truth serves to underscore something that should motivate all of us to right living:

It is for our benefit.

God tells us not to drink, for our benefit, not His. God tells us not to commit adultery for our benefit, not His. God tells us never to engage in homosexual behavior for our benefit, not His. God tells us to be faithful to church for our benefit, not His. God tells us to work and to save and to give for our benefit, not His. God commands women to be modest for their benefit, not His. God commands men not to lust for their benefit, not His. Whatever command God ever gives us will always ultimately be for our benefit, because He loves us!

So often, we struggle in the fight against sin. DO make good use of this arrow in that fight: living right is for my benefit!

Personal Notes:

_____

_____

_____

_____

_____

_____

_____

_____

_____

_____

_____

_____

_____

_____

_____

_____

_____

_____

_____

_____

_____

Devotion 38

Elihu will now give an excellent example of a great diagnosis and cure applied in all the wrong places and ways.

Job 35:9 *By reason of the multitude of oppressions they make the oppressed to cry: they cry out by reason of the arm of the mighty.* **10** *But none saith, Where is God my maker, who giveth songs in the night;* **11** *Who teacheth us more than the beasts of the earth, and maketh us wiser than the fowls of heaven?* **12** *There they cry, but none giveth answer, because of the pride of evil men.* **13** *Surely God will not hear vanity, neither will the Almighty regard it.*

Basically, Elihu is describing how wicked rich people oppress wicked poor people, and how even when those poor people cry against it, they receive no help, because they are not crying out to the God who could make everything better for them. Their pride keeps God from coming to their aid.

All of that is true, one hundred percent of it. And none of it accurately applies to Job, even though that is what Elihu was implying. Do you see, now, how easy it is to categorize people, make general statements of truth, and use truth as a weapon to destroy people who never should have been hit to begin with? We so crave for everything to be simple, black and white, quick answers, that we shove everything and everyone into handy categories, whether they entirely fit or not.

Categories can be helpful tools, but DO see individuals for who and what they are before you ever start contemplating categories!

Personal Notes:

_____

_____

_____

_____

_____

_____

_____

_____

_____

_____

_____

_____

_____

_____

_____

_____

_____

_____

_____

_____

_____

_____

_____

_____

_____

Devotion 39

Elihu's conclusion to this chapter is, to me, a bit maddening.

Job 35:14 *Although thou sayest thou shalt not see him, yet judgment is before him; therefore trust thou in him.* **15** *But now, because it is not so, he hath visited in his anger; yet he knoweth it not in great extremity:* **16** *Therefore doth Job open his mouth in vain; he multiplieth words without knowledge.*

If Elihu had stopped at verse fourteen, we could all shout a collective, "Thank you!" What better way to end a speech or part of a speech than by saying, "I know you are upset that you cannot see God, but God sees you, and he will handle all of this right, so just trust Him!" But Elihu has now joined the ranks of those who so skillfully snatch defeat from the jaws of victory. Right after telling Job to trust God, he goes on in verse fifteen to say, "But it isn't so; Job doesn't trust God. And because of that, God is really angry with him and is lowering the hammer on him, even though He could be making it worse." He now sounds exactly like Zophar, who said, *Know therefore that God exacteth of thee less than thine iniquity deserveth!*

Elihu, like the musketeers of misery before him, at this point either had no clue about the role that Satan played in all of this, or knew and would not say. Either way, while Job said some things about God that were not true, Elihu did as well. God was not angry with Job because of a lack of trust on Job's part. God trusted Job so much that He confidently held him up before Satan as the best of the best!

Should we encourage others to trust God? Absolutely. Can we help people to trust God by accusing them of not trusting Him when they do? No. It is like the modern "everything is racist" crowd, who produce racists by calling people who aren't racists racist. They produce what they claim to be fighting against because people get so angry at being unjustly labeled.

One of the best things we can ever do is help people to truly trust God. So DO avoid accusing people of not trusting Him unless it is very clear that they do not trust Him!

Personal Notes:

_____

_____

_____

_____

_____

_____

_____

_____

_____

_____

_____

_____

_____

Devotion 40

Elihu began with such promise. But the further he goes and the more he tries to set himself apart, the more he proves to be a mixed bag of wisdom and foolishness, humility and pomposity.

Job 36:1 *Elihu also proceeded, and said,* **2** *Suffer me a little, and I will shew thee that I have yet to speak on God's behalf.* **3** *I will fetch my knowledge from afar, and will ascribe righteousness to my Maker.* **4** *For truly my words shall not be false: he that is perfect in knowledge is with thee.*

In verse four, Elihu is actually addressing Job and saying, "Unlike these other three, you can now listen to me, one who is perfect in knowledge." There is simply no charitable way to spin that; it was amazingly arrogant. And what did this "perfect knowledge guy" proceed to deliver? Literally the exact same rehashed argument of the others:

Job 36:6 *He preserveth not the life of the wicked: but giveth right to the poor.* **7** *He withdraweth not his eyes from the righteous: but with kings are they on the throne; yea, he doth establish them for ever, and they are exalted.* **8** *And if they be bound in fetters, and be holden in cords of affliction;* **9** *Then he sheweth them their work, and their transgressions that they have exceeded.* **10** *He openeth also their ear to discipline, and commandeth that they return from iniquity.* **11** *If they obey and serve him, they shall spend their days in prosperity, and their years in* *pleasures.* **12** *But if they obey not, they shall perish by the sword, and they shall die without knowledge.* **13** *But the hypocrites in heart heap up wrath: they cry not when he bindeth them.* **14** *They die in youth, and their life is among the unclean.*

You could go back through the book of Job and find the three attackers of Job making all of these same claims, all of which amount to "God always blesses the righteous, and He always destroys the wicked." Can you just imagine how the three older men must have been looking on with mouths agape at Mr. "Perfect In Knowledge" at that moment?

If you are simply going to say what others have said, DO at least have the humility not to fancy yourself better than them as you do!

Personal Notes:

_____

_____

_____

_____

_____

_____

_____

_____

_____

_____

_____

_____

_____

Devotion 41

Elihu is now hell-bent on outdoing even what Job's first three attackers did. And he succeeds wildly.

Job 36:15 *He delivereth the poor in his affliction, and openeth their ears in oppression.* **16** *Even so would he have removed thee out of the strait into a broad place, where there is no straitness; and that which should be set on thy table should be full of fatness.* **17** *But thou hast fulfilled the judgment of the wicked: judgment and justice take hold on thee.* **18** *Because there is wrath, beware lest he take thee away with his stroke: then a great ransom cannot deliver thee.* **19** *Will he esteem thy riches? no, not gold, nor all the forces of strength.* **20** *Desire not the night, when people are cut off in their place.* **21** *Take heed, regard not iniquity: for this hast thou chosen rather than affliction.*

Elihu's assertion in these verses is that if Job had just done right, God would have stopped all the pain and made everything roses and unicorns for him. Then he closed this section of his argument by saying that, in wishing for death, Job was being wicked because he was just trying to find an easy way out of the punishment he was enduring for his sin.

May I remind you of something from much earlier in the book?

Job 2:8 *And he took him a potsherd to scrape himself withal; and he sat down among the ashes.*

Job was holding a razor-sharp item in his hand. He was in constant, excruciating pain; all of his children had died in a moment of time, his wife would not speak to him, and he had the means to end his own life. Yet he didn't. And here comes Elihu saying, "Yeah, but you WISHED for death, and that makes you wicked!"

There really should be times when it is okay to punch people.

Evaluating what people do or do not do as right or wrong based on what God has written is perfectly acceptable. But quibbling with hurting people's emotional wishes that they themselves clearly have no intention of acting on really is splitting some very fine hairs. DO give more grace than that; if Elihu knew everything YOU ever wished, he would probably have a bunch of snark to throw your way as well!

Personal Notes:

_____

_____

_____

_____

_____

_____

_____

_____

Devotion 42

Elihu is now in a pretty consistent pattern. When he speaks at all about Job, he blows it. But when he speaks about God, he does pretty well. He does not apply his knowledge of God correctly, but he at least has a fair concept of God's majesty. The next several verses will show that once again.

Job 36:22 *Behold, God exalteth by his power: who teacheth like him?* **23** *Who hath enjoined him his way? or who can say, Thou hast wrought iniquity?* **24** *Remember that thou magnify his work, which men behold.* **25** *Every man may see it; man may behold it afar off.* **26** *Behold, God is great, and we know him not, neither can the number of his years be searched out.* **27** *For he maketh small the drops of water: they pour down rain according to the vapour thereof:* **28** *Which the clouds do drop and distil upon man abundantly.* **29** *Also can any understand the spreadings of the clouds, or the noise of his tabernacle?* **30** *Behold, he spreadeth his light upon it, and covereth the bottom of the sea.* **31** *For by them judgeth he the people; he giveth meat in abundance.* **32** *With clouds he covereth the light; and commandeth it not to shine by the cloud that cometh betwixt.* **33** *The noise thereof sheweth concerning it, the cattle also concerning the vapour.*

After introductory statements in verses twenty-two through twenty-five, Elihu gets rolling in the right direction. In verse twenty-six, he points out that God is eternal. And then, in verses twenty-seven through thirty-three, he turns his attention to God's creation, specifically the clouds. Thousands of years ago, those who paid attention already understood the distillation process of clouds that is referenced in verse twenty-eight. The distillation process is a human-controlled version of the hydrological cycle (https://www.precisionwaterusa.com/blog/why-distillation). Elihu also noted how clouds spread, the noise of the thunder that comes from them, and the fact that the sun would be shining above the clouds while man was in darkness below the clouds. He concluded by pointing out that the cattle react differently as weather conditions change.

And all of this he correctly attributed to the hand of God.

We so often spend our days pining for miracles, heedless to the fact that we live in one. This world we live in is itself a miracle, one specifically designed to sustain life.

When you wake up each day and look out the window, DO whisper the word "miracle!"

Personal Notes:

_____

_____

_____

_____

_____

_____

Devotion 43

Elihu's mind is still in the clouds, as it were, and thankfully for the moment not in a bad way.

Job 37:1 *At this also my heart trembleth, and is moved out of his place. 2 Hear attentively the noise of his voice, and the sound that goeth out of his mouth. 3 He directeth it under the whole heaven, and his lightning unto the ends of the earth. 4 After it a voice roareth: he thundereth with the voice of his excellency; and he will not stay them when his voice is heard. 5 God thundereth marvellously with his voice; great things doeth he, which we cannot comprehend.*

All five of these verses are a very picturesque way to say that thunder is actually one of the ways that God speaks. In verse three, Elihu mentioned the lightning, that which first draws our attention, and then noted the thunder that comes after it. It is as if God grabs our attention with the flash and then speaks in His inutterable power. And before you pass this off as merely the superstition of ancient man who "did not understand that lightning discharge heats the air rapidly and causes it to expand," you might want to see this:

Revelation 10:3 *And cried with a loud voice, as when a lion roareth: and when he had cried, seven thunders uttered their voices. 4 And when the seven thunders had uttered their voices, I was about to write: and I heard a voice from heaven saying unto* *me, Seal up those things which the seven thunders uttered, and write them not.*

At least on this occasion, a human actually understood what thunder was saying! There are actually many instances in Scripture where thunder is regarded as being a literal voice. And why would God find it difficult to speak using thunder? He created sound, speech, and nature; He can speak however He likes.

Think about it. We go through literal storms, we see the lightning flash, we hear the thunder rumble, and it never occurs to us that, though we may not yet understand it, we have just heard the voice of God!

So, to brighten your day and remind you of the God who is still very much in charge over it all, the next time you hear the thunder rumble, DO smile and ask, "Is that you, Lord?"

Personal Notes:

_____

_____

_____

_____

_____

_____

_____

_____

_____

_____

Devotion 44

Continuing on with his look at nature and how it relates to the glory of God, Elihu will now speak of a few more aspects of the weather.

Job 37:6 *For he saith to the snow, Be thou on the earth; likewise to the small rain, and to the great rain of his strength.* **7** *He sealeth up the hand of every man; that all men may know his work.* **8** *Then the beasts go into dens, and remain in their places.* **9** *Out of the south cometh the whirlwind: and cold out of the north.* **10** *By the breath of God frost is given: and the breadth of the waters is straitened.*

Where modern man sees only the natural causes of snow, drizzle, and downpours, Elihu rightly attributes those "natural causes" to the God of nature, Who chooses all of those daily conditions. He then points out in verse seven that God uses the different weather to tell men when they can work and when they cannot. Even today, when the ice storm hits, the same thing holds true! Verse eight tells us that even the animals stop moving about when God uses the weather to tell them to stay home.

Verse nine relates to particular predictable weather patterns in that area of the world, patterns the ancients were well acquainted with. And then, in verse ten, Elihu ascribes even the simple frost to the breath of God and points out that said frost turns the water on the ground into a still, unmoving thing.

God uses the simple things of nature to accomplish His will. And man, for all of our modern technology and prowess, not only cannot produce any particular weather conditions, we are actually still just as much at the mercy of the weather as people were thousands of years ago!

So, the next time some aggressive atheist mocks God and your belief in Him to you, DO offer to loan him an umbrella since he has no more control over the rain than the cavemen he thinks he came from!

Personal Notes:

_____

_____

_____

_____

_____

_____

_____

_____

_____

_____

_____

_____

_____

_____

_____

_____

Devotion 45

Elihu is still speaking of the weather in relation to God's majesty. And were he to stop there, he would do well. But he won't.

Job 37:11 *Also by watering he wearieth the thick cloud: he scattereth his bright cloud:* **12** *And it is turned round about by his counsels: that they may do whatsoever he commandeth them upon the face of the world in the earth.* **13** *He causeth it to come, whether for correction, or for his land, or for mercy.*

Elihu describes in lovely, poetical terms how God takes the thick, strong clouds and simply says "rain," which then makes the cloud go away. It is His counsels that do this. And in verse thirteen, he semi-accurately points out that God uses the weather for correction or to bless His land or even for mercy. The reason I say "semi-accurately" is that Elihu missed something when he said this:

Matthew 5:45 *That ye may be the children of your Father which is in heaven: for he maketh his sun to rise on the evil and on the good, and sendeth rain on the just and on the unjust.*

This was Jesus pointing out what Elihu did not grasp. We cannot always infer from good weather or bad that God is either angry or pleased with anyone. Yes, the Scripture OFTEN gives us specific instances where God uses weather as a judgment or as a proof of favor, but He does not ALWAYS do so. And if

Elihu had understood that, he would not have then said this:

Job 37:14 *Hearken unto this, O Job: stand still, and consider the wondrous works of God.*

In other words, "Your hard times are proof of your sin, Job." New illustration, same old mistake.

We can legitimately know what is right or wrong based on what Scripture says. But we cannot conclusively know whether a person has done right or wrong based on circumstances in his or her life. So DO refrain from being an unqualified theological meteorologist!

Personal Notes:

_____

_____

_____

_____

_____

_____

_____

_____

_____

_____

_____

_____

_____

_____

_____

_____

Devotion 46

Once again, Elihu will reference nature in regard to God's majesty. And while he is still applying all of it wrong, the facts themselves are incredibly interesting.

Job 37:15 *Dost thou know when God disposed them, and caused the light of his cloud to shine?* **16** *Dost thou know the balancings of the clouds, the wondrous works of him which is perfect in knowledge?* **17** *How thy garments are warm, when he quieteth the earth by the south wind?*

Verse fifteen is a reference to the rainbow. Elihu understood that God somehow used the vapor of the clouds to produce the beauty of the rainbow, but he could not begin to fathom how God initially did all of it. His next question was about how clouds hang in the air. Adam Clarke paraphrased it this way, "How are the clouds suspended in the atmosphere? Art thou so well acquainted with the nature of evaporation, and the gravity of the air at different heights, to support different weights of aqueous vapour, so as to keep them floating for a certain portion of time, and then let them down to water the earth; dost thou know these things so as to determine the laws by which they are regulated?"[1] And then

---

[1] *Adam Clarke's Commentary of the Bible.* (n.d.). (Vol. 3). Abingdon-Cokesbury Press. p.165.

verse seventeen was an observation that when God brings in fair weather by the south wind, our clothes and we ourselves get warm. But it is in verse eighteen that things get really interesting:

Job 37:18 *Hast thou with him spread out the sky, which is strong, and as a molten looking glass?*

Houston, we have a problem. Does this verse teach the flat-earth, "We are living in a glass dome" theory? In short, no. Elihu has been talking about clouds for several verses, and he still is. The word "sky" in this verse is from the word *shachak*, and it means dust, cloud, thin cloud. In other words, when a huge sheet of bright clouds covers everything, as we look up, it becomes almost like a mirror. Those words "and as" are actually pretty important, too. They indicate a metaphor, not something to be taken literally. Our sky is not solid, and it is definitely not metal, as molten-looking glasses were in their days.

But it is glorious. All of it. And God did it just by the spoken word. And yet we, with all of our modern technology, cannot even begin to duplicate what He did and does!

DO remember that when it comes to the curve, we are the ones behind it, not God!

Personal Notes:

_____

_____

_____

_____

Devotion 47

Elihu will now utter his conclusion to Job, and it will be a mixture of sarcasm, accurate statements, and half-truths.

Job 37:19 *Teach us what we shall say unto him; for we cannot order our speech by reason of darkness.* **20** *Shall it be told him that I speak? if a man speak, surely he shall be swallowed up.* **21** *And now men see not the bright light which is in the clouds: but the wind passeth, and cleanseth them.* **22** *Fair weather cometh out of the north: with God is terrible majesty.* **23** *Touching the Almighty, we cannot find him out: he is excellent in power, and in judgment, and in plenty of justice: he will not afflict.* **24** *Men do therefore fear him: he respecteth not any that are wise of heart.*

The sarcasm I spoke of comes right up front in his conclusion, *teach us what we shall say unto him.* If you have been paying attention to Elihu at all, you know that he did not actually believe Job could teach him anything at all. His words at the end of verse nineteen further that sarcasm. They mean, "We are just so dumb, Job; our understanding is dark. Can you teach us, pretty please?"

From there, though, he gets a bit less pointed and more accurate. He points out in verses twenty and twenty-one that man really is pretty insignificant, so much so that he cannot see the sun that is hidden by the clouds until the clouds pass. Verse twenty-two is a bit of a "one is obvious and the other should be as well" kind of statement. Verse twenty-three is another true reminder that God is omnipotent and just, a thought that he basically restates in verse twenty-four. But the half-truth at the end of verse twenty-three is "he will not afflict," and in context, he means and says "unjustly." The reason it is a half-truth in this particular instance is that, while Elihu was right that God does not afflict unjustly, Job was afflicted unjustly, just not by God. Elihu, like the other three, believed that God had leveled Job, and therefore Job must have been unjust.

Elihu rushed in to help things, started well, veered off track, and never could quite get entirely back on course.

But he was done. Job's first three attackers were done, and now his fourth was done. And I find that pretty encouraging.

DO know that mouths do not run forever!

Personal Notes:

_____

_____

_____

_____

_____

_____

_____

_____

Devotion 48

For thirty-five chapters, we have heard from a man like Job, a man whom God called perfect and upright, yet who veered into error, in essence accusing God of behaving unfairly toward him. For thirty-five chapters, we have heard from men like Eliphaz, Zophar, and Bildad, who absolutely lied about Job in the most horrible of ways, accusing him of things like theft, murder, and child abuse. For thirty-five chapters, we have heard from a man like Elihu, who started well, trying to vindicate God, then fell into the same error of falsely accusing Job as the other three had, and even taking it farther than they had.

But as of chapter thirty-eight, everything will change. In chapter thirty-eight, the One person who knew and knows everything finally spoke up.

Job 38:1 *Then the LORD answered Job out of the whirlwind, and said,* **2** *Who is this that darkeneth counsel by words without knowledge?* **3** *Gird up now thy loins like a man; for I will demand of thee, and answer thou me.*

God could have appeared any way that He chose. But likely because the subject of clouds and weather had so very much been discussed, He appeared in a whirlwind and spoke out of it. And He spoke directly to Job. Please allow me to give you a spoiler alert here. While God immediately accused Job of speaking without knowledge, which was obviously completely true, do you know what He did not do a single time from here to the end of the book? He did not accuse Job of one thing wrong other than speaking wrong words about Him. No theft, no murder, no child abuse, and none of the other many accusations four men leveled against him. God's words, both at the beginning of the book and here at the end of the book, are proof positive that Job was innocent of all of their charges.

And Job never pushed back against a single thing God said to him. Since God got everything right, why should he? And since God always gets everything right, why should we? He said a lot of things Job did not want to hear, but He said nothing untrue. He will say a lot of things we do not want to hear, but He will say nothing untrue.

On days that you are tired of being unjustly accused, DO both take comfort and have a reverential fear over the fact that one day we will hear God speak to us face to face, and He will get absolutely everything right, whether we like it or not!

Personal Notes:

_____

_____

_____

_____

_____

_____

_____

Devotion 49

For the many chapters that God speaks, there will be one subject that He uses and draws truth from for Job to consider: nature. God speaks as the Creator to one of His creatures about His creation. And since He knows it all, these chapters are not just a theological treasure; they are also a scientific and cosmological treasure.

Job 38:4 *Where wast thou when I laid the foundations of the earth? declare, if thou hast understanding.* **5** *Who hath laid the measures thereof, if thou knowest? or who hath stretched the line upon it?* **6** *Whereupon are the foundations thereof fastened? or who laid the corner stone thereof;* **7** *When the morning stars sang together, and all the sons of God shouted for joy?*

The answer to God's first question to Job has an obvious answer; he wasn't even born yet. This world has foundations, God laid them, and Job was not there to see and therefore had no idea how He did it. The crust, which is all we have the ability to see, is five to twenty-five miles thick. The mantle beneath that is 1,800 miles thick. The outer core, which is 1,400 miles thick, lies beneath that. The very center, the inner core, is 800 miles thick. God did it; we did not see it, nor could we ever duplicate it.

Verse five means, "Who made everything just the right size and proportion as to actually function properly?" Our Earth hangs in its place, tilts just right, and rotates as it should because God made all of it the perfect size, shape, and composition. Verse six reminds us that we cannot see where the deepest foundations of the Earth are fastened, and that there was no human architect to lay a cornerstone of the Earth; God simply did it all Himself. Verse seven is a verse that peels back a bit of a heavenly veil for us. The morning stars and sons of God are terms used for angels. Angels saw all of this creative work as God did it and rejoiced and praised Him over it. This tells us that angels were created before the Earth was created. Whether that was a long time or mere seconds before, we do not know, but they were the witnesses to the six days of creation. It all kind of makes you want to say, "Wow!"

DO learn what Job learned; there is no one at all like our God!

Personal Notes:

_____

_____

_____

_____

_____

_____

_____

_____

_____

_____

Devotion 50

God, speaking from the whirlwind, continues to pepper Job with questions about creation, demonstrating His greatness. The last few verses dealt with the composition of the earth itself; the next few will deal with the sea.

Job 38:8 *Or who shut up the sea with doors, when it brake forth, as if it had issued out of the womb?* **9** *When I made the cloud the garment thereof, and thick darkness a swaddlingband for it,* **10** *And brake up for it my decreed place, and set bars and doors,* **11** *And said, Hitherto shalt thou come, but no further: and here shall thy proud waves be stayed?*

Verse eight gives us insight into the early seconds of creation. A few years ago, I watched an evolutionist explain how, in his view, the Earth came to be covered in water. He said, "One tiny drop at a time, carried by meteorites." Let that sink in: 332.5 million cubic miles of water got here one drop at a time on meteorites... So, since the meteorites are far bigger than the drops of water, where is all of that material? Obviously, since the water did not burn up on entry, neither did they!

That isn't how it happened. Verse eight tells us that God created all of it in an instant, and it came roaring into place like a baby expelled from the womb. And yet God "shut the doors on it," meaning He put it into place and then stopped it from going any farther. Verse nine tells us that it was all covered in thick clouds, and all of that was shrouded in darkness. Remember, light had not even been created yet!

In verses ten and eleven, He pictures Earth as if it were a castle of sorts, and has bars and doors designed to hold all of that water in its place. Even today, with all of our modern technology and equipment, we still cannot keep hurricanes and tsunamis from doing unfathomable damage. But God simply put water in place and said, "Stay where I put you," and it did!

There is nothing on earth more powerful than water, and yet God simply popped it out all at once, set boundaries for it, and smiled at His work. If God has enough control to do that, He has enough control to manage whatever is going on in your life as well. So DO grab a cold drink of water, and as you sip it, remind yourself that God has it all under control!

Personal Notes:

_____

_____

_____

_____

_____

_____

_____

_____

_____

_____

Devotion 51

God has questioned Job about the earth and about the sea, and He is just getting started. Now He will ask Job about something else he cannot comprehend: the sun.

Job 38:12 *Hast thou commanded the morning since thy days; and caused the dayspring to know his place;* **13** *That it might take hold of the ends of the earth, that the wicked might be shaken out of it?* **14** *It is turned as clay to the seal; and they stand as a garment.* **15** *And from the wicked their light is withholden, and the high arm shall be broken.*

Do you enjoy the sunrise each day? Job no doubt did so as well, at least before his body was wrecked. But at no time had Job ever "commanded" the morning. He had wished for it, and then at times wished against it, but it never paid the least bit of attention to him; it just did as God commanded it. The dayspring, by the way, means the sun. God asked Job if he was the one who caused it to know its place. Did he hang it? Did he make sure it shined exactly where and how it was supposed to? Did he, as verse thirteen shows, make it to shine on the activities of evil men who had been enjoying the cover of darkness, thereby making them scatter like roaches? Job knew the answer to all of that: nope.

In verse fourteen, God says that it, the Earth, is molded by the sun the way clay is by a seal when the seal is pressed into it. As the sun rises higher, shadows change, perception changes, and we see new things we had not seen just moments earlier. And they, those things, become like a lovely garment the earth wears.

Verse fifteen is both tricky and very cool. When the sun rises, the wicked person's "light" is taken away from him, so that his high arm, his power to do evil, is broken. In other words, the darkness is the evil person's "daytime," and real daytime takes it all away from him.

And Job had nothing to do with any of it and could not alter it in any way.

When the sun rises on each new day, DO remember that God ordained it and that He did so out of goodness to us; evildoers hate the light; therefore, a good God gives them what they hate and us what we love, all in the exact same sunrise!

Personal Notes:

_____

_____

_____

_____

_____

_____

_____

_____

_____

_____

Devotion 52

Continuing with a series of questions designed to make Job far more humble before the God he had, in his agony, spoken ill of, God moves now into asking Job about the sea and other aspects of creation.

Job 38:16 *Hast thou entered into the springs of the sea? or hast thou walked in the search of the depth?* **17** *Have the gates of death been opened unto thee? or hast thou seen the doors of the shadow of death?* **18** *Hast thou perceived the breadth of the earth? declare if thou knowest it all.* **19** *Where is the way where light dwelleth? and as for darkness, where is the place thereof,* **20** *That thou shouldest take it to the bound thereof, and that thou shouldest know the paths to the house thereof?* **21** *Knowest thou it, because thou wast then born? or because the number of thy days is great?*

Just in the first question of verse sixteen, we find a treasure house for the believer. God asked Job if he had entered into the springs of the sea. Not only had Job not walked in them, he did not even know they existed. In fact, modern scientists did not even discover them until very recently! It took the age of submarines for man to even become aware that there are springs in the bottom of the sea, water rising up from hydrothermal vents. So, no pun intended, "let that sink in." God knew about it, He had it written down in the book of Job, in the Bible, thousands of years ago, and mankind is just now getting "advanced" enough to even realize they exist. That is proof positive (as if we needed any) that God is real and that the Bible is the Word of God.

In verse seventeen, God asked Job if he had ever seen inside the world of the dead, even so much as just inside the gate. Then He asked him about the nature of light, which Job could no more explain than anything else God asked about. In verse twenty-one, He closed this section of thought by asking Job if he was old enough to have been there when all of this was brought about, which he wasn't.

Do you know one of the most liberating phrases you will ever learn? "I don't know." It really helps us to remember that there is a God, and we aren't Him, so DO practice your "I don't knows" today!

Personal Notes:

_____

_____

_____

_____

_____

_____

_____

_____

_____

_____

_____

_____

Devotion 53

God has asked Job about the earth, the sea, the sun, the springs at the bottom of the sea, and now He will ask him about some things much colder.

Job 38:22 *Hast thou entered into the treasures of the snow? or hast thou seen the treasures of the hail,* **23** *Which I have reserved against the time of trouble, against the day of battle and war?*

We have heard all of our lives that there are no two snowflakes alike. Interestingly, there is actually an institute that has studied it. Their conclusion was that one snowflake is so incredibly complex, beyond imagination, that it would be impossible for there to ever be another one just like it. Out of trillions of trillions of snowflakes, God manages to make each one unique!

And then there is the stark whiteness of snow. It is so much the standard for whiteness that in Isaiah 1:18, God used it as a picture of how thoroughly He forgives our sin. But think about that: clear water evaporates into gray clouds and falls to the earth as white snow. Treasure indeed! Snow has been used for centuries for cooling and recreation, and even for building igloos.

And then God spoke of the treasures of the hail, and He specifically listed one of the things He had in mind by that. Throughout Scripture and history, God has used hail as heavenly projectiles, weapons against the enemies of His people. And He will do so again at least three more times during the Tribulation Period. God can take something as simple as frozen falling water and make a weapon so formidable that no technology of man can even remotely defend against it. And Job had never entered into any of this; he merely saw it and wondered at it.

The next time it snows or hails, DO smile and let this word of praise roll off of your lips: "Treasure!"

Personal Notes:

_____

_____

_____

_____

_____

_____

_____

_____

_____

_____

_____

_____

_____

_____

_____

_____

_____

_____

_____

_____

Devotion 54

After questioning Job about the snow and hail, God turned to a very quick question about the light. Quick, mind you, but definitely not easy.

Job 38:24 *By what way is the light parted, which scattereth the east wind upon the earth?*

Every single day, a very wonderful thing happens. We call it sunrise. Our sun is ninety-three million miles away, and it takes its light eight minutes to get to Earth. When we look up and see the sun, it looks orange to us. But it is much closer to blueish white. The reason it looks orange is because its rays have to travel through our atmosphere to reach our eyes. When it enters our atmosphere, it begins to be "parted" or broken up into useful pieces for us. Some of it is filtered out, and needfully so. Some of it hits our skin and helps to produce Vitamin D so that we can live. Some of it hits the plants and the ground and causes food to grow. Some of it hits clouds and raindrops and produces the beautiful rainbow. We could go on forever!

But God also pointed out that it is this light that causes the east wind to arise. If there were no sun, the Earth would be shrouded in darkness, freeze over, and there would be no wind. But as the sun heats our atmosphere, rising from the east, wind begins to flow, allowing our world to live. No wind, everything stagnates, temperature fluctuates by hundreds of degrees from one spot to the next, and all life dies.

And Job could not answer God when He asked him how all of this happens.

DO thank God for the sunrise; it is more profound than you can ever fully understand!

Personal Notes:

_____

_____

_____

_____

_____

_____

_____

_____

_____

_____

_____

_____

_____

_____

_____

_____

_____

_____

_____

_____

_____

_____

_____

Devotion 55

God now begins to question Job about the hydrological cycle, and His questions are both poetical and profound.

Job 38:25 *Who hath divided a watercourse for the overflowing of waters, or a way for the lightning of thunder;* **26** *To cause it to rain on the earth, where no man is; on the wilderness, wherein there is no man;* **27** *To satisfy the desolate and waste ground; and to cause the bud of the tender herb to spring forth?* **28** *Hath the rain a father? or who hath begotten the drops of dew?* **29** *Out of whose womb came the ice? and the hoary frost of heaven, who hath gendered it?* **30** *The waters are hid as with a stone, and the face of the deep is frozen.*

Verses twenty-five through twenty-seven are one long sentence, all talking about the rain. God "dividing the watercourse for the overflowing of waters" means that the rain comes down evenly; there is not a tiny line of raindrops in one spot and a three-foot wide solid gush falling a few feet away. This even distribution prevents the damage that would be done by a radically non-even rain. God also divides the way for the lightning that causes the thunder; He allows the charge to build up in the cloud, and then has that charge seek and find a path to the ground. Even today, scientists understand this is how it works, but they are still unclear about exactly why. Verses twenty-six through twenty-seven tell us that God causes the rain to fall even in desolate areas where people do not live. And if He didn't, the earth would become largely uninhabitable due to the loss of plant life and, therefore, the loss of oxygen produced.

In verses twenty-eight through twenty-nine, God poetically reminds Job that if the rain and dew and ice and frost have a father, it isn't man, it is God. He made it all. And then in verse thirty, He informs Job that even the sea becomes so covered in ice that it is as if it is hidden by a slab of stone. And Job, who lived in the Middle East and had obviously never been to either of Earth's poles, would have been utterly unaware of this. Once again, God was thousands of years ahead of man's learning and discovery.

All of this hydrological cycle allows there to be life on Earth. If any part of it were broken, Earth would be in deep trouble, and man along with it. And Job was not responsible for any of it, nor could he even explain it.

Whether it is sunny and the water is rising to form clouds, or it is cloudy and begins to rain so the sun can shine again, DO realize that every bit of it is consistently operating according to God's plan!

Personal Notes:

_____

_____

_____

_____

_____

Devotion 56

The next line of questioning that God peppered Job with gives us some of the most amazing verses to consider in all of the Bible.

Job 38:31 *Canst thou bind the sweet influences of Pleiades, or loose the bands of Orion?* **32** *Canst thou bring forth Mazzaroth in his season? or canst thou guide Arcturus with his sons?* **33** *Knowest thou the ordinances of heaven? canst thou set the dominion thereof in the earth?*

Pleiades is a constellation of seven visible stars that are in Orion, the second constellation mentioned in verse thirty-one. Arcturus and his sons is another name for Ursa Major, the Great Bear. Mazzaroth is a word that refers to the twelve signs of the Zodiac. In other words, thousands of years ago, they already had their names and their pictures, and all of them were given by God Himself! That which more modern man has corrupted and even worshipped, God put over our heads as what the late Dr. D. James Kennedy called "The Gospel In The Stars." And the last phrase of verse thirty-three takes us right back to God's promise in Genesis 1:14 that they would be for *signs, and for seasons, and for days, and years*.

Back in verse thirty-one, when God asked if Job could *bind the sweet influences of Pleiades* (which he couldn't), it refers to the fact that they rise in spring and thus herald the coming of new growth on the earth.

In short, God made all of the stars over our heads, appointed them to inform man of both spiritual and seasonal truth, named all of them, appointed what pictures they would represent, and mankind still is guided by them today, even though many will never admit that God did it all.

DO go outside and see the stars sometime soon, and whisper, "My God did all of that!"

Personal Notes:

_____

_____

_____

_____

_____

_____

_____

_____

_____

_____

_____

_____

_____

_____

_____

_____

_____

Devotion 57

God is still questioning Job, and Job still has no answers. Now, the subject will again turn to the clouds.

Job 38:34 *Canst thou lift up thy voice to the clouds, that abundance of waters may cover thee?* **35** *Canst thou send lightnings, that they may go, and say unto thee, Here we are?* **36** *Who hath put wisdom in the inward parts? or who hath given understanding to the heart?* **37** *Who can number the clouds in wisdom? or who can stay the bottles of heaven,* **38** *When the dust groweth into hardness, and the clods cleave fast together?*

In verse thirty-four, God pointed out a problem that still plagues even modern man today with all of our technological prowess. No one can cause it to rain, no matter how badly that rain is needed! Man still looks up at the sky in agony as the crops wither and die, and the clouds will not drop their life-giving moisture.

In verse thirty-five, God points out that to us, lightning is random and uncontrollable, but to Him, they are directable and answerable! The old quip "God's gonna strike you with lightning!" is more than an idle threat; it is a very real possibility if needed!

Having given Job a lot to think about already, in verse thirty-six, God quickly turns Job's thoughts toward thinking! His question is basically, "How is it that you are able to think? Who caused that? How did it come to be?" Even today, listening to evolutionists try to explain this conundrum is hilarious. How does something like "thinking" ever evolve from "non-thinking?"

And then in verses thirty-seven and thirty-eight, God asks Job how droughts occur. Who causes that? Who makes a natural cycle like rain simply stop for three and a half years as it did in Elijah's day? Job experienced all of it: rain, lightning, thinking, and drought. But he could not explain or duplicate any of it.

This world is always looking for something supernatural, and they do not even recognize it as it happens each day. DO recognize that all of our "natural" is very much supernatural!

Personal Notes:

_____

_____

_____

_____

_____

_____

_____

_____

_____

_____

_____

_____

Devotion 58

As God brings His words in chapter thirty-eight to an end, He will begin to question Job about the animal kingdom. He will continue that line of questioning into the next chapter as well. Here is the set of questions He begins with:

Job 38:39 *Wilt thou hunt the prey for the lion? or fill the appetite of the young lions,* **40** *When they couch in their dens, and abide in the covert to lie in wait?* **41** *Who provideth for the raven his food? when his young ones cry unto God, they wander for lack of meat.*

In verses thirty-nine and forty, God asks Job about how lions manage to be fed. Somehow, they have an instinct in them that is perfect for hunting and stalking prey. How did that happen? It could not have "evolved over millions of years" because if it were not fully present in the very first generation of lions, they would all have starved and died out. But who put it there? How does it work? God did all of it, yet even though Job understood that he had no idea how God did it or how it works.

In verse forty-one, God asked about the same thing in regard to the ravens. These birds have a voracious appetite; they constantly need to be fed. So how do they even survive? How do they make it through the early hours and days of life? How did God arrange it for them to be fed in their helplessness and then to wander as far afield as necessary to find food once they are able? Again, it could not have "evolved over millions of years" because if it was not fully present in the very first generation of ravens, they would all have starved and died out. But who put it there? How does it work? God did all of it, yet even though Job understood that he had no idea how God did it or how it works.

The natural world is proof of the wisdom and majesty of God, so DO stand in awe of the God who made it all!

Personal Notes:

_____
_____
_____
_____
_____
_____
_____
_____
_____
_____
_____
_____
_____
_____
_____
_____
_____
_____

Devotion 59

As chapter thirty-nine begins, God is still questioning Job about different creatures in the animal kingdom. He dealt with the lions and ravens, and now He will ask Job about wild goats.

Job 39:1 *Knowest thou the time when the wild goats of the rock bring forth? or canst thou mark when the hinds do calve?* **2** *Canst thou number the months that they fulfil? or knowest thou the time when they bring forth?* **3** *They bow themselves, they bring forth their young ones, they cast out their sorrows.* **4** *Their young ones are in good liking, they grow up with corn; they go forth, and return not unto them.*

The first question God posed to Job dealt not with a general season in which wild goats bear young but with the exact moment each of them does so. The reason Job could not know that is because these splendid animals inhabit high rocks and mountains that Job could never climb! And yet God knows the exact moment and the exact spot that every single one of them gives birth.

The second question God asked was whether or not Job could tell how long they would be pregnant and also how long they live; both are wrapped up in God's question about months. And the reason He asked that was because they are both pregnant for a decent while for an animal, five months or so, and also live a very long time, thirty-five years or so! Job could never keep track of either their age or their gestational length, but God could and did.

Verse three describes their moment of birth. Then in verse four, God describes how they are strong very early on, learn to eat from the field without the help of man, and then shortly go on their way and never return. God programmed all of this into them. And Job could vaguely know what they do, but he could never know how God made it all work generation after generation, and he could never be there to see it high on the rocky mountains each time it began.

Goats. God even watches over the goats high on the barren mountain. So you, Mr. or Mrs. Introvert, DO know that God also watches over you as well!

Personal Notes:

_____

_____

_____

_____

_____

_____

_____

_____

_____

_____

_____

_____

_____

Devotion 60

Having questioned Job about the wild goat, God now turns His attention and line of questioning to the wild ass.

Job 39:5 *Who hath sent out the wild ass free? or who hath loosed the bands of the wild ass? 6 Whose house I have made the wilderness, and the barren land his dwellings. 7 He scorneth the multitude of the city, neither regardeth he the crying of the driver. 8 The range of the mountains is his pasture, and he searcheth after every green thing.*

The wild ass of the Middle East is a fast, stubborn, independent creature, and he is like that because God made him that way. God made him to live out in the wilderness and in barren lands that few other creatures could survive in. He scorns the city, and unlike the tame ass who is controlled (more or less) by the voice and urgings of the driver, he will not be. The horse needs a pasture to survive; to the wild ass, even the mountain is a pasture. This is possible because, as verse nine says, *he searcheth after every green thing.* In other words, he does not have to be particular in what he eats; his stomach is designed to handle almost anything.

Job heard all of this, Job knew all of this, and Job also knew that he had nothing to do with it and could not begin to explain how God brought it into being.

Think about that. We often use the phrase "dumb donkey," but we do not know how God made them like they are. So, who exactly are the dummies?

So the next time you feel proud, DO look in the mirror, point at your reflection, and say, "Hee-aw, Hee-aw, He awt to not be like that!"

Personal Notes:

_____

_____

_____

_____

_____

_____

_____

_____

_____

_____

_____

_____

_____

_____

_____

_____

_____

_____

_____

_____

_____

_____

Devotion 61

Having queried Job about lions, ravens, wild goats, and wild asses, God now asks him about a creature that inaccurately brings up visions of sparkles and rainbows in our minds.

Job 39:9 *Will the unicorn be willing to serve thee, or abide by thy crib?* **10** *Canst thou bind the unicorn with his band in the furrow? or will he harrow the valleys after thee?* **11** *Wilt thou trust him, because his strength is great? or wilt thou leave thy labour to him?* **12** *Wilt thou believe him, that he will bring home thy seed, and gather it into thy barn?*

The unicorn. Believe me, Bible haters love seeing this word pop up in Scripture! They mockingly accuse us of believing in fairy tales and refusing to grow up. But the problem is theirs, not ours, because believers are not the ones who started drawing cutesy-looking white horses with a golden horn and labeling them as unicorns!

The word unicorn simply means "one-horned creature." And the description is pretty clearly of a creature that we all know very well, a massive, strong beast with one major horn as its defining feature, the rhinoceros. As Job heard God ask him if he could make this creature serve him, stay peacefully in the barn, and plow the field for him, he must have shaken his head. No, Job could not do any of that, and he knew it. He also could not, as verses eleven and twelve describe, domesticate that beast and trust him to obey commands.

So, who made such a mighty, untamable creature? God did. What did Job have to do with that? Nothing. How much of it could Job explain? None of it.

For a man who proudly proclaimed that he wanted to talk to God face to face, when the questions started rolling in, Job got very, very quiet.

If we cannot explain the power of the rhino, we should not barge about as if we were rhinos.

DO blunt the tip of your horn; a little humility goes a long way with God!

Personal Notes:

_____
_____
_____
_____
_____
_____
_____
_____
_____
_____
_____
_____
_____
_____
_____

Devotion 62

Having previously questioned Job about ravens, God now asks him about two other birds, two birds that are wildly different from each other.

Job 39:13 *Gavest thou the goodly wings unto the peacocks? or wings and feathers unto the ostrich?* **14** *Which leaveth her eggs in the earth, and warmeth them in dust,* **15** *And forgetteth that the foot may crush them, or that the wild beast may break them.* **16** *She is hardened against her young ones, as though they were not hers: her labour is in vain without fear;* **17** *Because God hath deprived her of wisdom, neither hath he imparted to her understanding.* **18** *What time she lifteth up herself on high, she scorneth the horse and his rider.*

God asks Job exactly one question about the peacock, and the answer is clearly "no." The peacock has the most gorgeous, spectacular feathers on earth, and man did not cause them, nor did evolution. God made them.

But then comes the ostrich. The ostrich is careless. Many ostriches will leave their eggs lying on the ground, barely covered, and then will oftentimes even forget where she has put them. They are often then trampled accidentally or even broken intentionally by wild beasts. The ostrich is also calloused; ostriches are prone to lay a whole lot of eggs together from different females. That results in a situation where, oftentimes, she does not even recognize her young as her own, and she will become hardened against them. And it is God who has thus "deprived her of understanding."

In verse eighteen, we find that she is contemptuous. The people of the Middle East were fascinated by the ostrich and often attempted to capture them. But an ostrich can run more than forty-five miles per hour and can keep very near that speed for twenty solid minutes! So, when an ostrich gets chased by some guy on horseback, it can look back, stick its tongue out, and simply put the pedal to the metal!

God did all of this, and Job did not know how. He made a bird that no man could make if they would, or would make if they could. Why? Because He is God, and He likes it that way.

If you ever have your own universe, you can do everything your way. But since you don't, DO let God be God to you personally as He does everything His way!

Personal Notes:

_____

_____

_____

_____

_____

_____

_____

Devotion 63

Continuing with His line of questioning about the animal kingdom, God now turns his attention to questioning Job about the horse.

Job 39:19 *Hast thou given the horse strength? hast thou clothed his neck with thunder?* **20** *Canst thou make him afraid as a grasshopper? the glory of his nostrils is terrible.* **21** *He paweth in the valley, and rejoiceth in his strength: he goeth on to meet the armed men.* **22** *He mocketh at fear, and is not affrighted; neither turneth he back from the sword.* **23** *The quiver rattleth against him, the glittering spear and the shield.* **24** *He swalloweth the ground with fierceness and rage: neither believeth he that it is the sound of the trumpet.* **25** *He saith among the trumpets, Ha, ha; and he smelleth the battle afar off, the thunder of the captains, and the shouting.*

For ninety-nine percent or so of human history, the horse has been the greatest weapon on the battlefield. It was unchallenged as such until somewhere around the twentieth century, when the internal combustion engine provided us with things like tanks and airplanes. The horse continued to be used in warfare until after World War I! So, when God spoke to Job about the horse, there was a sense of awe in the ears of the hearers.

The description God gives in these verses is of a creature that is not only not afraid of battle, he is anxious for it. The horse is strong, fast, powerful, angry, and unafraid. Horses can weigh up to two thousand pounds, they can be as much as seven feet tall, can run up to forty-four miles per hour, jump over eight feet high, and their kicks travel at two hundred miles per hour and hit with a force of two thousand pounds per square inch. In short, they can easily kill you and then calmly graze beside your dead body.

Job had a sense of all of this, though he likely did not know all of the numbers. And he also knew that he had nothing to do with it, could not possibly explain any of it, and had challenged the God who did it simply by uttering the words *Let the earth bring forth the living creature after his kind, cattle, and creeping thing, and beast of the earth after his kind.*

God speaks, and horses instantly appear. Man spends thousands of years tinkering with what God has made and manages to get real dogs to produce lesser dogs like chihuahuas. Kind of puts things in perspective, doesn't it!

Don't horse around with God; DO give Him the respect He deserves!

Personal Notes:

_____

_____

_____

_____

_____

_____

_____

Devotion 64

Previously, God questioned Job about the peacock and the ostrich. Now He will question him about two more birds: the hawk and the eagle.

Job 39:26 *Doth the hawk fly by thy wisdom, and stretch her wings toward the south?* **27** *Doth the eagle mount up at thy command, and make her nest on high?* **28** *She dwelleth and abideth on the rock, upon the crag of the rock, and the strong place.* **29** *From thence she seeketh the prey, and her eyes behold afar off.* **30** *Her young ones also suck up blood: and where the slain are, there is she.*

Beginning with the hawk in verse twenty-six, God asks Job how a hawk manages to fly and how she understands to fly south when the weather gets colder. Where did that ability come from, and where did that instinct come from? She has no calendar and no cell phone alarm telling her it is time to do so.

Then God begins to question Job about the eagle, the most majestic of all birds. He mentions her "mounting up," meaning to take flight high into the sky. And they do; bald eagles fly as high as ten thousand feet. Then God mentioned her nesting on high, and again, she does. The eagle will nest in trees eighty-five to one hundred feet off the ground, some of which are on mountains standing several miles high! And her nests will be as much as thirteen feet by eight feet and weigh more than a ton!

God then spoke of her ability to see prey a great way off. An eagle can spot a rabbit from more than two miles away and pick it out from its camouflaged background when a human being might miss it from just a few feet away. In verse thirty, God mentioned that she is a predator, and her young have that trait from their earliest days as well.

And Job had no idea how any of this came to be, nor could he duplicate it.

If God can make a bird that can see a rabbit from two miles away, DO believe that God can also see you from His throne in Heaven!

Personal Notes:

_____
_____
_____
_____
_____
_____
_____
_____
_____
_____
_____
_____
_____
_____
_____
_____

Devotion 65

After an entire chapter of God alone speaking, we now come to our very first conversation between God and Job, initiated by God Himself.

Job 40:1 *Moreover the LORD answered Job, and said,* **2** *Shall he that contendeth with the Almighty instruct him? he that reproveth God, let him answer it.*

Let me remind you of the claims that Job had boldly made throughout the book:

Job 10:2 I *will say unto God, Do not condemn me; shew me wherefore thou contendest with me.*

Job 13:3 *Surely I would speak to the Almighty, and I desire to reason with God.*

Job 23:4 *I would order my cause before him, and fill my mouth with arguments.*

Job was really sure that if he ever had a face-to-face meeting with God, he would confidently argue with Him. And now, God was actually offering him that opportunity! So, how would he respond?

Job 40:3 *Then Job answered the LORD, and said,* **4** *Behold, I am vile; what shall I answer thee? I will lay mine hand upon my mouth.* **5** *Once have I spoken; but I will not answer: yea, twice; but I will proceed no further.*

Well, now, that doesn't sound much like "filling one's mouth with arguments," now does it! Job, a man that God Himself described as a perfect and upright man, saw himself as utterly vile once he found himself in the presence of God and had no more desire to speak at all. Let that sink in. The very best of the best, a man who was still being spoken of in Scripture thousands of years later as a wonderful example, saw himself as dirty and unworthy when he came face to face with God.

This says something about us, yes, but it says even more about God. God is, first and foremost, holy. He is so utterly pure that even our very best human version of "pure" is filthy by comparison! His wisdom is so far above ours that, even when we think we have everything figured out, just a few facts falling from His lips can render us speechless.

DO have a proper view of God; any view of God that somehow brings Him down to our level is not a proper view!

Personal Notes:

_____
_____
_____
_____
_____
_____
_____
_____
_____
_____
_____
_____

Devotion 66

God had offered Job a chance to argue. Job had wisely declined. But lesson number two was about to commence.

Job 40:6 *Then answered the LORD unto Job out of the whirlwind, and said,* **7** *Gird up thy loins now like a man: I will demand of thee, and declare thou unto me.* **8** *Wilt thou also disannul my judgment? wilt thou condemn me, that thou mayest be righteous?* **9** *Hast thou an arm like God? or canst thou thunder with a voice like him?* **10** *Deck thyself now with majesty and excellency; and array thyself with glory and beauty.* **11** *Cast abroad the rage of thy wrath: and behold every one that is proud, and abase him.* **12** *Look on every one that is proud, and bring him low; and tread down the wicked in their place.* **13** *Hide them in the dust together; and bind their faces in secret.* **14** *Then will I also confess unto thee that thine own right hand can save thee.*

God began this challenge in nearly the same words as the first. And then, in verse eight, He got to the crux of the current matter. Though Job was correct in stating that he had done nothing wrong prior to his life falling apart, he had swerved into wrong during his calamity by implying that God was wrong in how He dealt with Job. Job believed that if he was righteous, God must therefore be unrighteous. And that was not and never will be the case, no matter what happens in our lives.

In verses nine through thirteen, God reminds Job again of His omnipotence. Job could never hope to be as powerful as God, yet he had challenged God anyway. But it is in verse fourteen that we come to a golden nugget of theology. God said that if Job could do all of that, *Then will I also confess unto thee that thine own right hand can save thee.*

Save thee. Job needed salvation! In this case, it was not spiritual salvation but physical salvation that was being spoken of. But only God can provide either! Only He can save us from attacks of Satan, and only He can save our souls. There is an entire spiritual world that our flesh of this physical world can neither touch nor impact nor alter, and we therefore desperately need someone from that world to save us.

The weapons of our warfare are not carnal; DO cry out to the God who walks in both worlds to deal with the world that you cannot!

Personal Notes:

_____

_____

_____

_____

_____

_____

_____

_____

_____

_____

Devotion 67

As God continues His second set of questions to Job, we come to one of the coolest passages in the entire Bible. Let me give you the verses and then teach you something about them.

Job 40:15 *Behold now behemoth, which I made with thee; he eateth grass as an ox.* **16** *Lo now, his strength is in his loins, and his force is in the navel of his belly.* **17** *He moveth his tail like a cedar: the sinews of his stones are wrapped together.* **18** *His bones are as strong pieces of brass; his bones are like bars of iron.* **19** *He is the chief of the ways of God: he that made him can make his sword to approach unto him.* **20** *Surely the mountains bring him forth food, where all the beasts of the field play.* **21** *He lieth under the shady trees, in the covert of the reed, and fens.* **22** *The shady trees cover him with their shadow; the willows of the brook compass him about.* **23** *Behold, he drinketh up a river, and hasteth not: he trusteth that he can draw up Jordan into his mouth.* **24** *He taketh it with his eyes: his nose pierceth through snares.*

Many commentaries and study Bibles say that these verses refer to the elephant. But take another look at verse seventeen. I'll wait...

Do you see it? What elephant has a tail like a cedar tree?!? No, this is not an elephant. This creature ate grass, had strong loins (legs and hips), a huge, strong belly, *the sinews of his stones are wrapped together*, meaning he had powerful thighs, and his bones were as strong as brass and iron. He lived near the water's edge and was so massive that he believed he could drink up the entire river. His nose was so strong he could push it right through any snares set for him.

Elephant, no. Dinosaur, yes! This is something along the lines of a brontosaurus or apatosaurus. And it was alive during Job's day, just a few thousand years ago! This is a first-hand, historical account of it; Job knew about what God was describing in his present-tense reality.

DO know that you can trust your Bible, even in matters of the age of the earth, even when modern secular scientists (with a pre-decided agenda) say otherwise!

Personal Notes:

_____

_____

_____

_____

_____

_____

_____

_____

_____

_____

_____

Devotion 68

God used the last ten verses of chapter forty to question Job about a dinosaur that lived in the days of Job, one that they called Behemoth. And as if that was not remarkable enough, He will use all of chapter forty-one, all thirty-four verses, to describe another dinosaur, this time one called Leviathan. And this one was not just zoological knowledge; it also carried spiritual significance that other chapters of Scripture bear witness to.

Here is how God began to broach the subject with Job.

Job 41:1 *Canst thou draw out leviathan with an hook? or his tongue with a cord which thou lettest down?* **2** *Canst thou put an hook into his nose? or bore his jaw through with a thorn?* **3** *Will he make many supplications unto thee? will he speak soft words unto thee?* **4** *Will he make a covenant with thee? wilt thou take him for a servant for ever?* **5** *Wilt thou play with him as with a bird? or wilt thou bind him for thy maidens?* **6** *Shall the companions make a banquet of him? shall they part him among the merchants?* **7** *Canst thou fill his skin with barbed irons? or his head with fish spears?*

Leviathan was a dinosaur of the sea, a watery dragon of the deep. God asked Job if he could catch him with a hook like some kind of fish or even penetrate his head with fish spears. And Job knew that he could not. This creature, this ancient swimming dragon, seems to have been the fiercest creature on earth. So much so that he became a symbol of another incredibly fierce creature:

Isaiah 27:1 *In that day the LORD with his sore and great and strong sword shall punish leviathan the piercing serpent, even leviathan that crooked serpent; and he shall slay the dragon that is in the sea.*

This was a dual reference to Babylon and to Satan. Leviathan was so fearsome that the greatest enemies of God and His people became known as Leviathans. Job had to shudder when God asked of this creature; he had challenged God and yet trembled before a sea dragon, daring not to wade out into the deep where it might devour him.

Before you ever challenge God, DO ask yourself if you are capable of handling a sea dragon. If you aren't, then don't challenge the God who so easily made and manages such creatures!

Personal Notes:

_____

_____

_____

_____

_____

_____

_____

_____

_____

Devotion 69

As God continues His description of Leviathan, a sea dinosaur, a dragon in the water, we find some of the most fascinating facts about this creature, especially in light of the common, cringeworthy view that this was a crocodile. Behold:

Job 41:8 *Lay thine hand upon him, remember the battle, do no more.* **9** *Behold, the hope of him is in vain: shall not one be cast down even at the sight of him?* **10** *None is so fierce that dare stir him up: who then is able to stand before me?*

Verse eight means, "Just go put your hand upon him to start trouble. He will give you trouble you will never forget!" Verse nine tells us that just the sight of him is enough to make people give up. Verse ten says that he is so fierce that no one ever dares to stir him up. Steve Irwin, anyone? Definitely not a crocodile.

Job 41:13 *Who can discover the face of his garment? or who can come to him with his double bridle?*

The first phrase means, "Who can strip off his hide?" The second phrase is a reference to him having two rows of teeth. Verse fifteen goes on to say that *his scales are his pride.* When you see fictional stories of dragons gloating about their scales, it comes from reality! But verses nineteen through twenty-one are the most fascinating parts of the whole description:

Job 41:19 *Out of his mouth go burning lamps, and sparks of fire leap out.* **20** *Out of his nostrils goeth smoke, as out of a seething pot or caldron.* **21** *His breath kindleth coals, and a flame goeth out of his mouth.*

Yes, Virginia, there were indeed fire-breathing dragons in Earth's history. The legends and myths come from reality. But while man would run in terror at the sight of any real dragon, God did not. Look at what He said in verse eleven:

Job 41:11 *Who hath prevented me, that I should repay him? whatsoever is under the whole heaven is mine.*

DO be confident today; your God owns all dragons: past, present, and future!

Personal Notes:

_____

_____

_____

_____

_____

_____

_____

_____

_____

_____

_____

_____

_____

Devotion 70

As God continues to quiz Job about a creature that once roamed the earth, Leviathan, we find more descriptions of how fierce this creature was. It is clear that God saved the biggest and baddest for last, to drive home to Job just how mighty He, God, was. Everyone on Earth was scared of this thing; God wasn't.

Job 41:22 *In his neck remaineth strength, and sorrow is turned into joy before him.* **23** *The flakes of his flesh are joined together: they are firm in themselves; they cannot be moved.* **24** *His heart is as firm as a stone; yea, as hard as a piece of the nether millstone.* **25** *When he raiseth up himself, the mighty are afraid: by reason of breakings they purify themselves.* **26** *The sword of him that layeth at him cannot hold: the spear, the dart, nor the habergeon.* **27** *He esteemeth iron as straw, and brass as rotten wood.* **28** *The arrow cannot make him flee: slingstones are turned with him into stubble.* **29** *Darts are counted as stubble: he laugheth at the shaking of a spear.* **30** *Sharp stones are under him: he spreadeth sharp pointed things upon the mire.* **31** *He maketh the deep to boil like a pot: he maketh the sea like a pot of ointment.* **32** *He maketh a path to shine after him; one would think the deep to be hoary.* **33** *Upon earth there is not his like, who is made without fear.* **34** *He beholdeth all high things: he is a king over all the children of pride.*

It is apparent that this sea dragon often came onto land; we find him "raising up" and men trying to fight him with swords, spears, darts, habergeons (armor and lances), arrows, and slings. What a monster this must have been! He simply laughed at all of man's weapons. And when he went back into the water, he could make it boil (v.31). And God closed out His description of him by saying, *Upon earth there is not his like, who is made without fear. He beholdeth all high things: he is a king over all the children of pride.*

Dragon. This was an actual dragon. Man, of course, added the "wings and flying" part, but Leviathan was very real. And yes, dragons have always, even in stories, been regarded as kings over evil men (children of pride).

And yet God was unfazed. Job finally got the message; DO realize that God is bigger and greater than we can ever imagine!

Personal Notes:

_____

_____

_____

_____

_____

_____

_____

_____

_____

Devotion 71

We finally arrive at the pinnacle of the book, the place where Job "gets it."

Job 42:1 *Then Job answered the LORD, and said,* **2** *I know that thou canst do every thing, and that no thought can be withholden from thee.* **3** *Who is he that hideth counsel without knowledge? therefore have I uttered that I understood not; things too wonderful for me, which I knew not.* **4** *Hear, I beseech thee, and I will speak: I will demand of thee, and declare thou unto me.* **5** *I have heard of thee by the hearing of the ear: but now mine eye seeth thee.* **6** *Wherefore I abhor myself, and repent in dust and ashes.*

God asked Job who it was that was hiding or darkening counsel without knowledge. Job now answers: "It was me." He then, using the formal speech of a debate, proclaims himself the loser of said debate: *Hear, I beseech thee, and I will speak: I will demand of thee, and declare thou unto me. I have heard of thee by the hearing of the ear: but now mine eye seeth thee. Wherefore I abhor myself, and repent in dust and ashes.*

Throughout the book, Job knew how lofty he was, but he did not know how lofty God was. And when he finally saw how lofty God was, he realized how low his own loftiness was by comparison! And it is no mistake that this happens immediately after God proclaims Leviathan, the dragon, to be the "king over all the children of pride." It is as if He is saying, "Job, I am your king, but your pride is making it look like the dragon is actually your king!"

If you have ever really gotten to know God, everyone will be able to tell it because you will be very, very humble. DO truly get to know Him; it would be a shame for a child of the King to somehow find himself in his pride kneeling at the scaly feet of the dragon!

Personal Notes:

_____

_____

_____

_____

_____

_____

_____

_____

_____

_____

_____

_____

_____

_____

_____

_____

_____

_____

Devotion 72

When last we heard from Job, he had apologized to God for his ill-advised words. That was all God wanted to hear from Job. But God was not done yet; there were some others he wanted to speak to about... Job.

Job 42:7 *And it was so, that after the LORD had spoken these words unto Job, the LORD said to Eliphaz the Temanite, My wrath is kindled against thee, and against thy two friends: for ye have not spoken of me the thing that is right, as my servant Job hath.* **8** *Therefore take unto you now seven bullocks and seven rams, and go to my servant Job, and offer up for yourselves a burnt offering; and my servant Job shall pray for you: for him will I accept: lest I deal with you after your folly, in that ye have not spoken of me the thing which is right, like my servant Job.*

This was the sweetest moment of vindication for Job. In assault after assault after assault, his three adversaries said the most horrible things about him. Imagine the jaw-dropping moment when they heard God call Job "my servant" three times! And then God required them to humble themselves before Job and get Job to pray for them. Only then could they escape God's judgment. And I will say more about that entire scene in the next devotion. For now, just focus on the fact that God vindicated Job. And it may surprise you to know that this is not the last time He did so:

148

Ezekiel 14:14 *Though these three men, Noah, Daniel, and Job, were in it, they should deliver but their own souls by their righteousness, saith the Lord GOD.*

Ezekiel 14:20 *Though Noah, Daniel, and Job, were in it, as I live, saith the Lord GOD, they shall deliver neither son nor daughter; they shall but deliver their own souls by their righteousness.*

James 5:11 *Behold, we count them happy which endure. Ye have heard of the patience of Job, and have seen the end of the Lord; that the Lord is very pitiful, and of tender mercy.*

In short, Eliphaz, Bildad, and Zophar were dead wrong and under the wrath of God. Elihu started right, then ended up just as wrong, but God seems to have not been quite as angry with him since he was the youth in the group and since he at least got a few things right. But Job, flaws and all, ends up fully, verbally vindicated by God, and then gets glorious mentions hundreds and even thousands of years later by God through the pens of Ezekiel and James.

Whenever you are getting savaged unjustly, DO be patient, because God will eventually bring everything to light!

Personal Notes:

_____

_____

_____

_____

Devotion 73

To review something we saw in the last devotion, here is what God said to Eliphaz and Company when He spoke to them:

Job 42:7 *And it was so, that after the LORD had spoken these words unto Job, the LORD said to Eliphaz the Temanite, My wrath is kindled against thee, and against thy two friends: for ye have not spoken of me the thing that is right, as my servant Job hath.* **8** *Therefore take unto you now seven bullocks and seven rams, and go to my servant Job, and offer up for yourselves a burnt offering; and my servant Job shall pray for you: for him will I accept: lest I deal with you after your folly, in that ye have not spoken of me the thing which is right, like my servant Job.*

That had to be a gut punch for these three hateful peacocks. But they really had little choice in the matter. Job, though, did have a choice! So, what would he do with it?

Job 42:9 *So Eliphaz the Temanite and Bildad the Shuhite and Zophar the Naamathite went, and did according as the LORD commanded them: the LORD also accepted Job.* **10a** *And the LORD turned the captivity of Job, when he prayed for his friends...*

You are Job, and you have been falsely accused of child abuse, stealing from widows, and many other horrible things. Then you find out that if you do not pray for the people who lied about you, God is going to whack them. Be honest; aren't you very much tempted to say, "Let me see if I can get around to that. I think I may have some time right after I finish hand-picking every dandelion on the planet..."

But Job did not do that. Knowing that their fate was in his hands, he actually prayed and asked God to spare them. Job was more spiritual than I am, I fear. What about you? But when Job prayed for them, God did not just spare them; he also restored Job! And God had not at any point told Job that that was the way it would work; Job just prayed for them because it was the right thing to do.

DO be willing to pray, even for those who have hurt you; ultimately, it is more for your benefit than for theirs!

Personal Notes:

_____

_____

_____

_____

_____

_____

_____

_____

_____

_____

_____

_____

Devotion 74

When last we saw Job, who had been hideously attacked by his "friends," he prayed for them. And what happened next was like a dump truck load of the Balm of Gilead:

Job 42:10 *And the LORD turned the captivity of Job, when he prayed for his friends: also the LORD gave Job twice as much as he had before.* **11** *Then came there unto him all his brethren, and all his sisters, and all they that had been of his acquaintance before, and did eat bread with him in his house: and they bemoaned him, and comforted him over all the evil that the LORD had brought upon him: every man also gave him a piece of money, and every one an earring of gold.* **12** *So the LORD blessed the latter end of Job more than his beginning: for he had fourteen thousand sheep, and six thousand camels, and a thousand yoke of oxen, and a thousand she asses.* **13** *He had also seven sons and three daughters.*

The Lord gave Job twice as much in material goods as he had before. Seven thousand sheep was now fourteen thousand, three thousand camels was now six thousand, five hundred oxen was now a thousand, and five hundred she asses was now a thousand. In children, though, Job, who had lost all ten of his precious children, went on to have exactly ten more. You see, children are not "possessions;" they are a parent's most precious gifts of God, whose loss can never be fully gotten over. And God would not cheapen that by saying, "Here is two for one, you can feel better now."

Additionally, all of the friends and family who had abandoned Job in his hour of need came back to comfort him and even brought gifts. But that begs a question, doesn't it? Why did they wait until things were better to do that? All of that would have meant so much more if they had done it when he actually needed it most!

What we do is important; WHEN we do it is equally important! DO give your flowers (real flowers, encouragement, visits, calls, texts, cards, help) when people need it most, rather than waiting until they are better or dead!

Personal Notes:

_____

_____

_____

_____

_____

_____

_____

_____

_____

_____

_____

_____

_____

_____

Devotion 75

As the description of the restoration of Job continues, we find something that seems so unusual in its context but is really beautiful and instructive.

Job 42:13 *He had also seven sons and three daughters.* **14** *And he called the name of the first, Jemima; and the name of the second, Kezia; and the name of the third, Kerenhappuch.* **15** *And in all the land were no women found so fair as the daughters of Job: and their father gave them inheritance among their brethren.*

It is clear that Job's estranged relationship with his wife was fully repaired; they had ten more children. But concerning these children, all of these verses focus on the daughters of Job; the names of the sons are not even mentioned! To this day, we have no idea what the name of any of Job's sons was. But before we even begin to consider the names of Job's daughters, notice that it was Job himself who named them. We are told so often (mostly by Bible-haters who have never bothered to read what they so badly hate) that women in the Bible were afterthoughts or "property." But Job personally named all three of his daughters. Jemima meant *daylight*, the perfect name for a daughter whose father just went through the darkest of nights. Kezia was named after the cassia plant, a sweet and aromatic herb, the perfect name for the daughter of a man who had previously had foul breath and rotting flesh. Kenrenhappuch meant *horn of stibium*, a makeup that women of those days used on their eyes, a perfect name for the daughter of a man whose flesh had lost all beauty.

Verse fifteen tells us that they were the most beautiful women in all the land. They were a lovely living testimony that God disagreed with the vile things his attackers had famously said of him. And Job gave these precious girls an inheritance along with the boys, a very unusual occurrence in the world of those days. Once again, God's people led the way in the proper treatment of women!

These girls were the glory of their father. Daughters of any age, DO remember that everything about you reflects on your father, both your earthly father and your heavenly Father!

Personal Notes:

_____
_____
_____
_____
_____
_____
_____
_____
_____
_____
_____
_____
_____

Devotion 76

We now come to the "the end" of the book of Job. And when you really think about it, these simple words make for a very excellent "the end."

Job 42:16 *After this lived Job an hundred and forty years, and saw his sons, and his sons' sons, even four generations.* **17** *So Job died, being old and full of days.*

After this lived Job... in our modern wording, we would say, "After this, Job lived." In fact, he lived for 140 more years and saw his kids give him a crop of grandkids, and then his grandkids gave him great-grandkids, and then his great-grandkids gave him great-great-grandkids. But it is in the words "after this Job lived" that we find a treasure.

After this; after Job had the very worst day of his life, he went on living. After this; after burying ten children, he went on living. After this; after he went bankrupt, he went on living. After this; after his wife stopped speaking to him, he went on living. After this; after his health was completely decimated, he went on living. After this; after being savagely attacked and lied about, he went on living. After this; after the devil himself did his worst to wreck Job, he went on living. After this; after Elihu seemed to offer hope and then turned on a dime and cut him even deeper than the others, he went on living. After this; after Job wished repeatedly for death, he went on living. After this; after Job held a razor-sharp object in his hands that could have ended his life but did not use it for that, he went on living.

Job hurt and suffered more than any man who ever lived. But his story ended happily because, when he could not figure out anything else to do, he just kept on living and kept on living for God.

Sometimes, just opening your eyes to another sunrise is a victory in and of itself.

When life gets so hard that you don't know what to do, DO keep on living, and DO keep on living for God. Happy endings start right there!

Personal Notes:

_____

_____

_____

_____

_____

_____

_____

_____

_____

_____

_____

_____

_____

_____

_____

_____

_____

Devotion 77

And now we enter the glorious book of Psalms—if we can refer to 150 songs whose subject matter ranges from praise to war to clinical depression, glorious!

And we can. The Psalms are often gritty, sometimes way too real, frequently encouraging, but always instructive. Psalms is the Hebrew hymn book, if you will, and the characters and writers of the New Testament quoted from it or alluded to it more than one hundred times.

Psalm 1:1 *Blessed is the man that walketh not in the counsel of the ungodly, nor standeth in the way of sinners, nor sitteth in the seat of the scornful.* **2** *But his delight is in the law of the LORD; and in his law doth he meditate day and night.* **3** *And he shall be like a tree planted by the rivers of water, that bringeth forth his fruit in his season; his leaf also shall not wither; and whatsoever he doeth shall prosper.*

Psalm 1 presents us with a contrast, a choice we must make. We will either hang around the wicked or avoid them. Obviously, evangelism is not in view here; the subject is fellowship. And verses one through three give us a clear command and a subtle warning. The subtle warning is that getting around the wicked is a progressive matter; we go from walking by, to standing with, to sitting beside them. But the person who wishes to be blessed avoids all of that altogether! We must either delight ourselves in the

158

law of the LORD or delight ourselves in the company of sinners; we cannot possibly do both.

DO choose the path of blessing; choose to delight yourself in the law of the LORD and depart from the fellowship of the wicked!

Personal Notes:

_____

_____

_____

_____

_____

_____

_____

_____

_____

_____

_____

_____

_____

_____

_____

_____

_____

_____

_____

_____

_____

_____

_____

_____

Devotion 78

The last half of Psalm 1 completes the contrast between sinners and the righteous and gives us even more reason to hang out with the righteous instead of the wicked.

Psalm 1:4 *The ungodly are not so: but are like the chaff which the wind driveth away.* **5** *Therefore the ungodly shall not stand in the judgment, nor sinners in the congregation of the righteous.* **6** *For the LORD knoweth the way of the righteous: but the way of the ungodly shall perish.*

Unlike the righteous, who are likened in verse three to a tree planted by the rivers of water, the ungodly are like powdery chaff which is blown away by the wind. The further contrast in verse five is that the ungodly will not be able to stand at judgment day and will not enter into the congregation of the righteous, meaning Heaven. Verse six concludes by saying that the LORD "knows" the way of the righteous, meaning He gives it official recognition. But the way of the ungodly shall perish; God will never place His stamp of approval on it.

Simply put, sinners and the righteous are on two entirely different pathways, and we, the righteous, are to keep to our designated pathway! The saved cannot go to hell, but they can absolutely be wrecked in this life and lose rewards in eternity for walking the pathway of and with the wicked or for trying to have one foot on their pathway and one foot on ours.

DO keep to the pathway that keeps you out of ungodly trouble and have nothing to do with the pathway that gets you into ungodly trouble!

Personal Notes:

_____

_____

_____

_____

_____

_____

_____

_____

_____

_____

_____

_____

_____

_____

_____

_____

_____

_____

_____

_____

_____

_____

_____

Devotion 79

Though many Bibles do not list it as such, Acts 4:25 clearly marks Psalm 2 as a Psalm of David. David wrote around half of the Psalms, and this one is filled with war, prophecy, and theology.

Psalm 2:1 *Why do the heathen rage, and the people imagine a vain thing?* **2** *The kings of the earth set themselves, and the rulers take counsel together, against the LORD, and against his anointed, saying,* **3** *Let us break their bands asunder, and cast away their cords from us.* **4** *He that sitteth in the heavens shall laugh: the Lord shall have them in derision.* **5** *Then shall he speak unto them in his wrath, and vex them in his sore displeasure.* **6** *Yet have I set my king upon my holy hill of Zion.*

When you see the LORD in all capital letters in the Old Testament, it is Jehovah God being referred to. That is a reference to the entire Godhead, the three-in-one God. But it is also often specifically a reference to either the Father or the Son. In this case, it is referring to the Father, because His "anointed" is referring to the Son, as we will see in the last half of the chapter.

The heathen, a word for the Gentiles, did indeed rage against the God of Israel. They were (and often still are) convinced that they could break God's authority that He has over them and be free to do whatever they like. But God was not and is not worried about their attempts; verse four tells us that

He laughs contemptuously at their feeble efforts, and will vex them on that account, and has set His King in place whether they like it or not.

When the world seems like they have successfully murdered God, DO remember that there is no reason to wring your hands in worry. God is very literally in heaven laughing at how ridiculous they are as He reaches for the divine paddle for their posteriors!

Personal Notes:

_____

_____

_____

_____

_____

_____

_____

_____

_____

_____

_____

_____

_____

_____

_____

_____

_____

_____

Devotion 80

The last six verses of Psalm 2 contain a very famous phrase of Scripture and a stern warning about "sweet, sweet Jesus."

Psalm 2:7 *I will declare the decree: the LORD hath said unto me, Thou art my Son; this day have I begotten thee.* **8** *Ask of me, and I shall give thee the heathen for thine inheritance, and the uttermost parts of the earth for thy possession.* **9** *Thou shalt break them with a rod of iron; thou shalt dash them in pieces like a potter's vessel.* **10** *Be wise now therefore, O ye kings: be instructed, ye judges of the earth.* **11** *Serve the LORD with fear, and rejoice with trembling.* **12** *Kiss the Son, lest he be angry, and ye perish from the way, when his wrath is kindled but a little. Blessed are all they that put their trust in him.*

Verse seven speaks of the "begotten" son of God. The most famous place this is ever mentioned is obviously John 3:16. But it is also specifically mentioned in Acts 13:33, Hebrews 1:5, and Hebrews 5:5. But since Jesus has always been, many people are really confused as to how He was ever "begotten." But as is always the case, Scripture is the best explainer of Scripture:

Acts 13:33 *God hath fulfilled the same unto us their children, in that he hath raised up Jesus again; as it is also written in the second psalm, Thou art my Son, this day have I begotten thee.*

Revelation 1:5 *And from Jesus Christ, who is the faithful witness, and the first begotten of the dead...*

Jesus was not begotten by birth; He was begotten by resurrection. Psalm 2 was a prophecy of that event. But it is in the very last verse that we find an even more surprising fact about Jesus when we read, *Kiss the Son, lest he be angry, and ye perish from the way, when his wrath is kindled but a little.* This was directed to the heathen who hate and oppose Him. Far from being the soft, feminine, placid Jesus created out of whole cloth by liberal seminaries, Jesus is capable of great anger.

DO know Jesus, but DO make sure the Jesus you know is actually the real Jesus!

Personal Notes:

_____
_____
_____
_____
_____
_____
_____
_____
_____
_____
_____
_____
_____

Devotion 81

Psalm 3 gives us insight into one of the most heartbreaking times of David's life. But it was heartbreaking primarily because of who the enemy was, not so much what the enemy did.

Psalm 3:1 <A Psalm of David, when he fled from Absalom his son.> *LORD, how are they increased that trouble me! many are they that rise up against me.* **2** *Many there be which say of my soul, There is no help for him in God. Selah.* [*This word indicates a musical pause, a time to reflect on what has just been sung.]

David's own son, Absalom, tried to destroy him. You will never know a greater hurt than having someone you love that much turn against you. But David found help, even for so deep a hurt as that:

Psalm 3:3 *But thou, O LORD, art a shield for me; my glory, and the lifter up of mine head.* **4** *I cried unto the LORD with my voice, and he heard me out of his holy hill. Selah.* **5** *I laid me down and slept; I awaked; for the LORD sustained me.* **6** *I will not be afraid of ten thousands of people, that have set themselves against me round about.*

David was on the run, in the wilderness, hiding in caves, and yet was able to sleep soundly. How? He turned all of his focus away from his problem and to the God Who could solve those problems. Mind you, the problems were huge; when David spoke in verse six of "ten thousands of people, that have set themselves against me," he was speaking literally, not metaphorically. But again, this was not an issue of counting noses; this was an issue of either looking out at his overwhelming troubles or looking up to the One for whom those troubles were child's play to deal with.

When you are facing the deepest of hurts and the biggest of problems, DO look up way more than you look out!

Personal Notes:

_____
_____
_____
_____
_____
_____
_____
_____
_____
_____
_____
_____
_____
_____
_____
_____
_____
_____

Devotion 82

Psalm 4 is an excellent study in the power of personal pronouns. As with Psalm 3, the prescript gives some historical context to the Psalm itself.

Psalm 4:1 <To the chief Musician on Neginoth, A Psalm of David.> *Hear me when I call, O God of my righteousness: thou hast enlarged me when I was in distress; have mercy upon me, and hear my prayer.*

Neginoth meant stringed instruments. David wrote this song and delivered it to his chief musician on those stringed instruments. It was written in a time of great distress, quite likely the same as that of chapter three, the rebellion of Absalom. Verse one is directed to God, but things change in verses two through five.

Psalm 4:2 *O ye sons of men, how long will ye turn my glory into shame? how long will ye love vanity, and seek after leasing? Selah. 3 But know that the LORD hath set apart him that is godly for himself: the LORD will hear when I call unto him. 4 Stand in awe, and sin not: commune with your own heart upon your bed, and be still. Selah. 5 Offer the sacrifices of righteousness, and put your trust in the LORD.*

All of these verses are directed to his enemies. By using "ye" three times along with several more understood pronouns, he made that very clear. Sometimes, addressing your enemies is absolutely necessary! But you do not need to ever get "stuck" there:

Psalm 4:6 *There be many that say, Who will shew us any good? LORD, lift thou up the light of thy countenance upon us. 7 Thou hast put gladness in my heart, more than in the time that their corn and their wine increased. 8 I will both lay me down in peace, and sleep: for thou, LORD, only makest me dwell in safety.*

David came through his trials because, while he addressed the enemy, he adored God. Even in the midst of being hunted and attacked, he simply could not help but cast his gaze to the God he loved so dearly and trusted so completely.

DO follow that pattern; address your enemy, but adore your God!

Personal Notes:

_____

_____

_____

_____

_____

_____

_____

_____

_____

_____

_____

_____

Devotion 83

The previous Psalm was designed for stringed instruments. The odd-sounding word Nehiloth in the prescript to this one lets us know it was likely for wind instruments:

Psalm 5:1 <To the chief Musician upon Nehiloth, A Psalm of David.> *Give ear to my words, O LORD, consider my meditation.*

The previous Psalm was designed as an evening Psalm; verse four said, *commune with your own heart upon your bed, and be still.* This Psalm is designed as a morning Psalm:

Psalm 5:3 *My voice shalt thou hear in the morning, O LORD; in the morning will I direct my prayer unto thee, and will look up.*

As to type, this Psalm is, among other things, an imprecatory Psalm. That simply means that it calls for harsh judgment on enemies. David will move from noting God's view of sin to predicting God's final dealing with sinners to actually calling for that final dealing on sinners. Notice that progression:

Psalm 5:4 *For thou art not a God that hath pleasure in wickedness: neither shall evil dwell with thee.*

Psalm 5:5 *The foolish shall not stand in thy sight: thou hatest all workers of iniquity.*

Psalm 5:10 *Destroy thou them, O God; let them fall by their own counsels; cast them out in the* *multitude of their transgressions; for they have rebelled against thee.*

So, is this okay? That would be a "yes." This is, after all, God that we are talking about, and the inspired Word of God as well. And what many squeamish believers miss is that since we are not allowed to take vengeance on the wicked, and since God has promised to do so (Romans 12:19), there is nothing at all wrong with us asking God to do what He has already promised to do! And doing so acts very much as a pressure relief valve for us; it allows us to blow off steam in the safest of environments.

DO take advantage of the right to pray imprecatory prayers; it is way better than life behind bars!

Personal Notes:

_____

_____

_____

_____

_____

_____

_____

_____

_____

_____

_____

_____

Devotion 84

We now come to another Psalm of David, this one with a musical notation we have already learned (Neginoth, stringed instruments) and a new one to go along with it.

Psalm 6:1 <To the chief Musician on Neginoth upon Sheminith, A Psalm of David.> *O LORD, rebuke me not in thine anger, neither chasten me in thy hot displeasure.*

Sheminith denotes a lower octave, a more mournful sound. And the content of the chapter fits well with that. David begins, right here in verse one, by asking God not to chasten and rebuke him in His hot displeasure. And verses two through seven do not get any more cheerful:

Psalm 6:2 *Have mercy upon me, O LORD; for I am weak: O LORD, heal me; for my bones are vexed.* **3** *My soul is also sore vexed: but thou, O LORD, how long?* **4** *Return, O LORD, deliver my soul: oh save me for thy mercies' sake.* **5** *For in death there is no remembrance of thee: in the grave who shall give thee thanks?* **6** *I am weary with my groaning; all the night make I my bed to swim; I water my couch with my tears.* **7** *Mine eye is consumed because of grief; it waxeth old because of all mine enemies.*

Whatever he had done, and whatever was going on, David was in such a bad way that he was certain that he was going to die if things did not change. His saddest words of all, though, were the words of verse four, *Return, O LORD*.

Return, O LORD.

If a person is having to ask for God to come back, then things have gotten very bad indeed! And while we know that the Holy Spirit indwells the believer forever in the New Testament era, there is still a principle to be applied in our fellowship with God. God can and will feel very distant and unavailable to us when we allow sin and uncleanness into our lives. We can very quickly have the "soundtrack of our lives" go into a minor key if we do not live right.

You are largely in control of the soundtrack. DO live your life in C, not in A Minor!

Personal Notes:

_____

_____

_____

_____

_____

_____

_____

_____

_____

_____

_____

_____

_____

Devotion 85

We now arrive at the seventh Psalm, another Psalm of David. And, as in others, there is an interesting prescript.

Psalm 7:1 <Shiggaion of David, which he sang unto the LORD, concerning the words of Cush the Benjamite.> *O LORD my God, in thee do I put my trust: save me from all them that persecute me, and deliver me:*

Shiggaion indicates a sad song, a pleading song. And in this case, David was pleading with God because of some enemy he called Cush the Benjamite. And that provides us with a fun mystery. You see, there was no Cush mentioned anywhere in the life or times of David! But there was another man whose actions toward David matched what we see in this Psalm, namely, King Saul. And Saul had a father whose name, both in English and Hebrew, was almost identical to Cush, namely Kish. This Psalm is almost certainly a veiled reference to Saul trying to kill David, and likely written while David was actually on the run. And that would explain why he used a subtle code instead of coming right out and naming his enemy; he didn't need any more trouble than he already had!

The next few verses show what David was facing and on what basis he asked to be delivered:

Psalm 7:2 *Lest he tear my soul like a lion, rending it in pieces, while there is none to deliver.* **3**

O LORD my God, if I have done this; if there be iniquity in my hands; 4 If I have rewarded evil unto him that was at peace with me; (yea, I have delivered him that without cause is mine enemy:) 5 Let the enemy persecute my soul, and take it; yea, let him tread down my life upon the earth, and lay mine honour in the dust. Selah.

David was facing a horrible death. And his basis for asking God to deliver him was that he had not done any of what Saul was accusing him of; in fact, he had spared Saul's life on multiple occasions! It must have been nice, from David's perspective, not to have to waste precious time starting his prayer like this: "Lord, I know I really did wrong, but if you would please forgive me because I really need it..." No, he could just go straight to "Help!"

DO live your life in such a way that when you go to God seeking help, you do not have to waste a lot of time explaining yourself or apologizing for your own idiocy or iniquity!

Personal Notes:

_____

_____

_____

_____

_____

_____

_____

_____

Devotion 86

As David continues asking God to preserve him, we come to some verses that give us tremendous insight into the spiritual state of the nation at that point in time.

Psalm 7:6 *Arise, O LORD, in thine anger, lift up thyself because of the rage of mine enemies: and awake for me to the judgment that thou hast commanded.* **7** *So shall the congregation of the people compass thee about: for their sakes therefore return thou on high.* **8** *The LORD shall judge the people: judge me, O LORD, according to my righteousness, and according to mine integrity that is in me.* **9** *Oh let the wickedness of the wicked come to an end; but establish the just: for the righteous God trieth the hearts and reins.*

Verse six takes us back in time to when Samuel, at God's direction, anointed David as the next king. This was the "judgment that God had commanded." David was asking for it to come to be. But verse seven then tells us why this was so important to David. It had nothing to do with palace or prosperity; it had to do with the fact that under David's reign, the people would be taught to make God the center of life, while that was not the case under Saul. Verses eight and nine continue in that vein, showing the difference between the righteous and the wicked and asking God to establish the former and remove the latter.

No wonder David was called the man after God's own heart. If a man can look at the crown and desire it only to be an influence for God, he really is exactly what God is looking for.

Whoever you are, whatever your position in life, DO look at advancements in position mainly through the lens of "What will it help me do for God?' rather than through the lens of "What can I personally get out of this?"

Personal Notes:

_____

_____

_____

_____

_____

_____

_____

_____

_____

_____

_____

_____

_____

_____

_____

_____

_____

_____

_____

Devotion 87

As David closes out this Psalm by asking God for help against the man who is trying to kill him, he will make a very shocking statement.

Psalm 7:10 *My defence is of God, which saveth the upright in heart.* **11** *God judgeth the righteous, and God is angry with the wicked every day.* **12** *If he turn not, he will whet his sword; he hath bent his bow, and made it ready.* **13** *He hath also prepared for him the instruments of death; he ordaineth his arrows against the persecutors.* **14** *Behold, he travaileth with iniquity, and hath conceived mischief, and brought forth falsehood.* **15** *He made a pit, and digged it, and is fallen into the ditch which he made.* **16** *His mischief shall return upon his own head, and his violent dealing shall come down upon his own pate.* **17** *I will praise the LORD according to his righteousness: and will sing praise to the name of the LORD most high.*

Under the inspiration of God, in verse eleven, David said, *God is angry with the wicked every day!* He then went on to describe how, if the wicked man did not change, God would come against him with sword, bow, arrows, and other instruments of death. And, far from being unrighteous for God to feel this way, David ascribed all of this to the righteousness of God in verse seventeen and praised God for it.

So, what are we to do with this?

Believe it. God is indeed angry with the wicked every day. And yet, He also loved the wicked enough to die for them and offers each day to save them. No one can balance that quite like God does! And if God were not angry with the wicked, if He were perfectly fine with the wicked abusing and destroying the righteous, He would not be a holy God at all, merely a theological cuddly stuffed animal of no value in our hour of need.

DO praise God for everything, including His righteous anger toward the wicked!

Personal Notes:

_____

_____

_____

_____

_____

_____

_____

_____

_____

_____

_____

_____

_____

_____

_____

_____

Devotion 88

In Psalm 7, the subject matter was judgment. But in Psalm 8, it turns to the subject of highest joy:

Psalm 8:1 <To the chief Musician upon Gittith, A Psalm of David.> *O LORD our Lord, how excellent is thy name in all the earth! who hast set thy glory above the heavens.* **2** *Out of the mouth of babes and sucklings hast thou ordained strength because of thine enemies, that thou mightest still the enemy and the avenger.* **3** *When I consider thy heavens, the work of thy fingers, the moon and the stars, which thou hast ordained;* **4** *What is man, that thou art mindful of him? and the son of man, that thou visitest him?* **5** *For thou hast made him a little lower than the angels, and hast crowned him with glory and honour.* **6** *Thou madest him to have dominion over the works of thy hands; thou hast put all things under his feet:* **7** *All sheep and oxen, yea, and the beasts of the field;* **8** *The fowl of the air, and the fish of the sea, and whatsoever passeth through the paths of the seas.* **9** *O LORD our Lord, how excellent is thy name in all the earth!*

Psalms 81 and 84 also start with this mention of Gittith. It means *of the winepress*. In other words, it was a song designed to be sung at a time of joy and celebration. And it was. The Gittith Psalms were sung at the Feast of Booths, one of the happiest times of the year.

David's circumstances are not mentioned in the Psalm simply because our circumstances are not the source of real joy; the excellency of God is the source of real joy. God's very name is excellent in all the earth; both the first and last verses show us that. And the verses in between show us the glory of the universe He has made (vs. 1b- 3) and the dominion that that amazing God has given man (vs. 4-8). And all of this is so wonderful that this Psalm is one of the most commonly quoted ones in the New Testament. Simply put, we have a lot to be joyful about because of how great our God is in and of Himself (His person) and how good He has chosen to be to us (His presents).

DO rejoice in the excellency of God's person and presents!

Personal Notes:

_____

_____

_____

_____

_____

_____

_____

_____

_____

_____

_____

_____

_____

_____

Devotion 89

As Psalm 9 begins, we find yet another prescript, this one even more mysterious than all of the previous ones.

Psalm 9:1 <To the chief Musician upon Muthlabben, A Psalm of David.> *I will praise thee, O LORD, with my whole heart; I will shew forth all thy marvellous works.*

What in the world is Muthlabben? Well, it is, first of all, a compound word. The first part of it, *muwth*, means *death*. So, right off the bat, we know this is going to be interesting! The second part is from the word bane, or *ben* in our tongue, and it means *son*. So this is a Psalm about the death of some important son. And interestingly, an ancient Chaldee text says, "concerning the death of the Champion who went out between the camps." That was a reference to Goliath, the favored son and hometown hero of Gath! This Psalm, then, very much seems to have been written concerning David's great victory over that giant. And he begins it by saying, *I will praise thee, O LORD, with my whole heart; I will shew forth all thy marvellous works.*

Interesting; no "I'm the greatest!" like Muhammad Ali; no "Everybody has a plan till they get punched in the mouth" like Mike Tyson; no crowing or boasting in anything except the marvelous works of God. And he continues in that vein throughout the Psalm:

Psalm 9:2 *I will be glad and rejoice in thee: I will sing praise to thy name, O thou most High.* **3** *When mine enemies are turned back, they shall fall and perish at thy presence.*

This again fits perfectly with 1 Samuel 17. The Philistines were coming toward Israel, then turned and ran when their hero fell. And far from ascribing that to his own prowess, David attributed it to the presence of God. No wonder God gave David so much success and so many victories; David was very good at remembering where all of those successes and victories came from.

If you want to be more successful, DO start with remembering Who our victories come from!

Personal Notes:

_____

_____

_____

_____

_____

_____

_____

_____

_____

_____

_____

_____

Devotion 90

As David continues his muthlabben Psalm, he both addresses the Philistines and gives great theological truth about the throne and character of God.

Psalm 9:4 *For thou hast maintained my right and my cause; thou satest in the throne judging right.* **5** *Thou hast rebuked the heathen, thou hast destroyed the wicked, thou hast put out their name for ever and ever.* **6** *O thou enemy, destructions are come to a perpetual end: and thou hast destroyed cities; their memorial is perished with them.* **7** *But the LORD shall endure for ever: he hath prepared his throne for judgment.* **8** *And he shall judge the world in righteousness, he shall minister judgment to the people in uprightness.*

In verse four, David rejoices that God viewed him and his cause as right and gave him the victory. This was God "judging right," as he put it. In verse six, he speaks of his enemies destroying entire cities, which they were famously known to do, but he also reminded them that that had now come to an end. But then, in verse seven, David spoke of God on His throne yet again, and in verse eight, reminded everyone that God judges in uprightness.

But it is the word *minister* that makes verse eight so interesting. The judgment that God "administers" truly is a "ministry!" It certainly was for David, who rightly saw a giant fall.

We often fear God's judgment. But it would DO us well to remember that it is as much ministry as it is administered!

Personal Notes:

_____

_____

_____

_____

_____

_____

_____

_____

_____

_____

_____

_____

_____

_____

_____

_____

_____

_____

_____

_____

_____

_____

_____

_____

Devotion 91

Davis is still singing about the righteous judgment of God. And as in the previous verses, he paints that as a comfort for the righteous, not a concern.

Psalm 9:9 *The LORD also will be a refuge for the oppressed, a refuge in times of trouble.* **10** *And they that know thy name will put their trust in thee: for thou, LORD, hast not forsaken them that seek thee.* **11** *Sing praises to the LORD, which dwelleth in Zion: declare among the people his doings.* **12** *When he maketh inquisition for blood, he remembereth them: he forgetteth not the cry of the humble.*

As God on His throne looks with a disapproving eye toward those who oppress His people, He simultaneously acts as a refuge for His people in their oppression. And this is why David can confidently say in verse nine that those who know the name of the LORD will willingly put their trust in Him, because He never forsakes them. This then leads to the outward testimony of singing praises to the LORD and testifying of Him to others in verse eleven.

But in verse ten, we find an ominous-sounding note that is actually anything but: God makes inquisition for blood; He remembers the cry of those who have been hurt or killed. He also does not forget the cry of the humble, no matter what the humble is being put through by the wicked. Just like in the episode of Cain and Abel, God always eventually comes around asking all of the right questions.

Have you been hurt unjustly? DO know that God never sweeps that kind of thing under the rug. Instead, He turns over every single rock and discerns everything that is there, no matter how successful people may believe they have been at hiding it!

Personal Notes:

_____

_____

_____

_____

_____

_____

_____

_____

_____

_____

_____

_____

_____

_____

_____

_____

_____

_____

_____

_____

Devotion 92

As David continues his muthlabben Psalm, he expands the horizon of his thought.

Psalm 9:13 *Have mercy upon me, O LORD; consider my trouble which I suffer of them that hate me, thou that liftest me up from the gates of death:* **14** *That I may shew forth all thy praise in the gates of the daughter of Zion: I will rejoice in thy salvation.* **15** *The heathen are sunk down in the pit that they made: in the net which they hid is their own foot taken.* **16** *The LORD is known by the judgment which he executeth: the wicked is snared in the work of his own hands. Higgaion. Selah.*

In verse thirteen, David referenced the trouble he had experienced from those that hated him. And in a very short time from when he strode onto the battlefield, there was more than plenty of that: Eliab chewed him out in front of everyone, Goliath cursed him and tried to kill him, and then Saul started trying to kill him! And yet God protected him through it all. And one reason David was so grateful for that is because it allowed him to "show forth God's praise in the gates of the daughter of Zion," meaning the place where God's people gathered.

In verse fifteen, David harkened back to the heathen being sunk down in the pit they themselves made. The Philistines picked a fight, and they wrecked themselves in so doing. And David would see that time and again through the years. David references that thought again in verse sixteen when he said, *the wicked is snared in the work of his own hands.* This truth far exceeds just the immediate battle, and David knew it, which is why he started the verse with, *The LORD is known by the judgment which he executeth.*

As David ends that verse, he says, *Higgaion. Selah.* Those musical notations basically mean, "Bring it to a powerful crescendo, that pause so everyone can think on it."

It is easy to say that "God will deal with our enemies." But just saying it will never be as good as really emphasizing it and then truly meditating on it, so DO emphasize and meditate on it!

Personal Notes:

_____

_____

_____

_____

_____

_____

_____

_____

_____

_____

_____

_____

_____

Devotion 93

As David ends the ninth Psalm, he expands it exponentially in its reach and, in so doing, gives needed guidance not just to his people but to all the world.

Psalm 9:17 *The wicked shall be turned into hell, and all the nations that forget God.* **18** *For the needy shall not alway be forgotten: the expectation of the poor shall not perish for ever.* **19** *Arise, O LORD; let not man prevail: let the heathen be judged in thy sight.* **20** *Put them in fear, O LORD: that the nations may know themselves to be but men. Selah.*

Twice in just four verses, David mentions the nations. And far from being "an unbiblical construct that displeases God," as I have heard many supposedly Bible-believing leftists say, nations were actually God's idea:

Acts 17:26 *And hath made of one blood all nations of men for to dwell on all the face of the earth, and hath determined the times before appointed, and the bounds of their habitation;*

So God made the nations and even placed them where He wanted them and for as long as He wanted them. And that is why David's warning is so serious in this Psalm. Any nation that forgets the God who made them, any nation that forgets that they are just men and thus answerable to God, is ushering in their own destruction.

And this is why, as important as the military is, as important as the economy is, as important as education is, nothing is more important to the survival of a nation than the people of God. You, child of God, hold the key to the survival of this land! Just by winning souls and spreading the truth of Scripture on every subject, you are doing more to ensure the continued life of America than all of our generals and senators and businessmen put together.

DO bring the truth of God and Scripture to everyone everywhere in our land!

Personal Notes:

_____

_____

_____

_____

_____

_____

_____

_____

_____

_____

_____

_____

_____

_____

_____

_____

_____

_____

Devotion 94

The tenth Psalm's authorship is not certain, nor are the times or exact circumstances known. What is abundantly clear is that it is a Psalm of complaint; the author is being battered by enemies and seems to think that God is ambivalent toward his plight.

Psalm 10:1 *Why standest thou afar off, O LORD? why hidest thou thyself in times of trouble?* **2** *The wicked in his pride doth persecute the poor: let them be taken in the devices that they have imagined.* **3** *For the wicked boasteth of his heart's desire, and blesseth the covetous, whom the LORD abhorreth.* **4** *The wicked, through the pride of his countenance, will not seek after God: God is not in all his thoughts.* **5** *His ways are always grievous; thy judgments are far above out of his sight: as for all his enemies, he puffeth at them.* **6** *He hath said in his heart, I shall not be moved: for I shall never be in adversity.* **7** *His mouth is full of cursing and deceit and fraud: under his tongue is mischief and vanity.*

Verses two through six give complaint after complaint about the wicked. They persecute the poor, they are boastful, they are proud, they evict God from their thoughts, they have foul mouths, and they are dishonest. All of that is a formidable list, especially when it is directed at the righteous! But it is the complaint of verse one that is the most poignant; the psalmist feels like God knows what is going on but is keeping Himself at a distance and even hiding Himself when He is called on for help.

That is a bad place to get to in your own head. But most every believer arrives at that point at some time or another. The key is to never stay there, and the psalmist didn't.

Psalm 10:17 *LORD, thou hast heard the desire of the humble: thou wilt prepare their heart, thou wilt cause thine ear to hear:* **18** *To judge the fatherless and the oppressed, that the man of the earth may no more oppress.*

When you arrive at "GodDoesntCareVille," DO make sure you pass right on through to "GodDoesCareOpolis!"

Personal Notes:

_____

_____

_____

_____

_____

_____

_____

_____

_____

_____

_____

_____

_____

_____

_____

Devotion 95

We come to another Psalm of David in the eleventh Psalm. It is directed to David's chief music leader, and it is in two divisions of thought, verses one through three and verses four through seven.

Psalm 11:1 <To the chief Musician, A Psalm of David.> *In the LORD put I my trust: how say ye to my soul, Flee as a bird to your mountain?* **2** *For, lo, the wicked bend their bow, they make ready their arrow upon the string, that they may privily shoot at the upright in heart.* **3** *If the foundations be destroyed, what can the righteous do?*

This Psalm is widely regarded as being written when Saul was trying to kill David, and it does fit that situation well. But whether it was that circumstance or some other, the truth that it presents is the same. David's life was at risk, and people who meant well were telling him to run for his life and never look back. David's response, though, was that he would instead put his trust in the LORD and stand his ground. Mind you, he obviously did end up having to run at different times. But the stated reason for him to stand his ground as long as he could is, according to verse three, the fact that if the foundations are destroyed, the righteous can do nothing; they are helpless and hopeless. And while this rather famous verse is usually taken to mean that we need to take care of spiritual foundations for our own benefit, in the context, it meant something different when David wrote these words. You see, since Saul had long since given up being a suitable foundation for the people to stand on, David knew that he was the only option left. In this metaphor, David was actually the foundation. And if he crumbled, the righteous people of the land would have no firm foundation on which to stand.

When you feel like giving up, DO remember that there are countless people not just watching you but actually relying on you. Your courage may well be the foundation they find to stand upon in time of need!

Personal Notes:

_____

_____

_____

_____

_____

_____

_____

_____

_____

_____

_____

_____

_____

_____

_____

_____

_____

Devotion 96

While the first three verses of Psalm 11 were about David's determination to stand in the face of his wicked adversaries, the last four verses of the Psalm turn squarely to his confidence in what God will ultimately do to the wicked.

Psalm 11:4 *The LORD is in his holy temple, the LORD'S throne is in heaven: his eyes behold, his eyelids try, the children of men.* **5** *The LORD trieth the righteous: but the wicked and him that loveth violence his soul hateth.* **6** *Upon the wicked he shall rain snares, fire and brimstone, and an horrible tempest: this shall be the portion of their cup.* **7** *For the righteous LORD loveth righteousness; his countenance doth behold the upright.*

While David was determined to be a firm foundation on earth, he knew that his ultimate hope came from the One sitting on the throne in the Temple in Heaven. David reminded those hearing this Psalm that God does see what is happening and that He does draw a distinction between the righteous and the wicked. The LORD trieth (examines and proves) the righteous, but He simply hates the violence-loving wicked. Far from being tolerant, David said that God would rain snares and fire and brimstone and a horrible tempest down on the head of the wicked. And this is because, as verse seven says, that *the righteous LORD loves those who are righteous*. In other words, if God did not judge the wicked who were assaulting the righteous, He would not be loving toward the righteous.

People sometimes get a picture of God in their mind as someone who is laid-back and all-approving and non-offensive. And that picture does an injustice to the holy character of God and leaves the righteous with no confidence that God will deal with those who are unjustly assaulting them.

DO maintain a right view of God in your mind: a view that sees Him both as the advocate of the righteous and the enemy of the wicked!

Personal Notes:

_____

_____

_____

_____

_____

_____

_____

_____

_____

_____

_____

_____

_____

_____

_____

_____

_____

Devotion 97

Psalm 12 is the second and final Sheminith Psalm; the other one, which we have already covered, is Psalm 6. And this one, like that one, indicates a lower octave, a more mournful sound. And it only takes one verse for that sad sound to be heard in the lyrics as well:

Psalm 12:1 <To the chief Musician upon Sheminith, A Psalm of David.> *Help, LORD; for the godly man ceaseth; for the faithful fail from among the children of men.*

When a song starts with the word *Help*, there is an above-average chance that it is going to be a sad song. And when David goes on to say, *for the godly man ceaseth; for the faithful fail from among the children of men*, we easily see why he was troubled. For whatever reason, whether death or destruction or something else entirely, David was looking around day by day and seeing fewer and fewer godly and faithful people. And in their place, here is what he saw:

Psalm 12:2 *They speak vanity every one with his neighbour: with flattering lips and with a double heart do they speak.*

Where David once had seen godly and faithful men, now he saw more and more people whose words were characterized by vanity (hollow, empty promises), flattery (words of undeserved praise

198

designed solely to gain someone's favor), and double-heartedness (hypocrisy and double standards).

Think of what that means. David did not look to shouting or running or crying or any emotional display to determine if someone was righteous or wicked; he looked to their words. Jesus did as well:

Matthew 12:37 *For by thy words thou shalt be justified, and by thy words thou shalt be condemned.*

When someone's words are marked by all the wrong things, their polish or passion means nothing by comparison. DO make your words right, and DO make sure your actions match your words!

Personal Notes:

_____

_____

_____

_____

_____

_____

_____

_____

_____

_____

_____

_____

_____

_____

_____

Devotion 98

In verses one and two, David lamented the loss of good men and the growing number of evil men. And he especially focused on the speech of those evil men. He will do so again in the next three verses:

Psalm 12:3 *The LORD shall cut off all flattering lips, and the tongue that speaketh proud things: 4 Who have said, With our tongue will we prevail; our lips are our own: who is lord over us? 5 For the oppression of the poor, for the sighing of the needy, now will I arise, saith the LORD; I will set him in safety from him that puffeth at him.*

Verse three almost sounds truly hilarious if we take it wrong; *The LORD shall cut off all flattering lips, and the tongue that speaketh proud things.* If this meant that God would cut off our physical lips from our faces if we engaged in flattery, think of how flattery would sound going forward:

"Ooo awah a ood pu-uhn, ah wak ooo ewey uch..."

Fortunately for our ears, this phrase actually means something much worse; there will come a day and a point at which God takes the life of the person with flattering lips and a proud tongue. And while that may seem harsh, verse five shows us why it isn't; the wicked person uses his flattering lips and proud tongue to utterly destroy the righteous.

People used to say, "Sticks and stones may break my bones, but words will never hurt me!" Before you believe that, you might want to ask Joseph whether or not Mrs. Potiphar's words hurt him, and ask Daniel whether the lies of the other presidents in Persia hurt him, and even ask Jesus whether the betrayal of Judas hurt Him.

You have the power to build or to destroy with your words, to heal or to hurt. DO only speak words that the God of Heaven approves of!

Personal Notes:

_____

_____

_____

_____

_____

_____

_____

_____

_____

_____

_____

_____

_____

_____

_____

_____

_____

_____

Devotion 99

The last few verses of Psalm 12 give one of the most comforting promises to children of God, a promise that we can look through history and find to be absolutely, verifiably true.

Psalm 12:5 *For the oppression of the poor, for the sighing of the needy, now will I arise, saith the LORD; I will set him in safety from him that puffeth at him.* **6** *The words of the LORD are pure words: as silver tried in a furnace of earth, purified seven times.* **7** *Thou shalt keep them, O LORD, thou shalt preserve them from this generation for ever.*

In verse five, God spoke of the poor and needy, and He promised to arise and set him in safety from the enemy that was puffing at him, trying to destroy him. When He gave that promise, there were doubtless some oppressed Jews who wondered whether that promise could be counted on. So, God, in verse six, gave those people a good reason to trust Him, saying, *The words of the LORD are pure words: as silver tried in a furnace of earth, purified seven times*. In other words, if God says it, you can count on it. His words do not have the impurity of human error in them; they are like silver that has been absolutely impeccably purified seven times over. And what was it, again, that God promised those poor and needy? Only that, according to verse seven, Thou shalt keep them, O LORD, thou shalt preserve them from this generation forever.

Those words were written more than 3,000 years ago. And yet, despite attempted holocausts at the hands of Haman of Persia, Hitler of Germany, Stalin of Russia, and many more, God has faithfully preserved His people against all odds.

DO know that God's Word and words can be counted on!

Personal Notes:

_____

_____

_____

_____

_____

_____

_____

_____

_____

_____

_____

_____

_____

_____

_____

_____

_____

_____

_____

_____

_____

Devotionals

DO Drops Volume 1
DO Drops Volume 2
DO Drops Volume 3
DO Drops Volume 4
DO Drops Volume 5
DO Drops Volume 6
DO Drops Volume 7
DO Drops Volume 8
DO Drops Volume 9
DO Drops Volume 10
DO Drops Volume 11
DO Drops Volume 12

More Books by Dr. Bo Wagner

Beyond the Colored Coat
Don't Muzzle the Ox
From Footers to Finish Nails
I'm Saved! Now What???
Learning Not to Fear the Old Testament
Marriage Makers/Marriage Breakers
Why Christmas?
Colossians: The Treasures of Deity
Daniel: Breathtaking
Esther: Five Feasts and the Fingerprints of God
Ephesians: Treasures of Family
Galatians: Treasures of Liberty
Hosea: Love When It Matters Most
James: The Pen and the Plumb Line

Jonah: A Study in Greatness
Nehemiah: A Labor of Love
Proverbs: Bright Lights from Dark Sayings Vol 1
Proverbs: Bright Lights from Dark Sayings Vol 2
Romans: Salvation From A-Z
Ruth: Diamonds in the Darkness
The Revelation: Ready or Not

Books in the Night Heroes Series

Cry From the Coal Mine (Vol. 1)
Free Fall (Vol. 2)
Broken Brotherhood (Vol. 3)
The Blade of Black Crow (Vol. 4)
Ghost Ship (Vol. 5)
When Serpents Rise (Vol. 6)
Moth Man (Vol. 7)
Runaway (Vol. 8)
Terror by Day (Vol. 9)
Winter Wolf (Vol. 10)
Desert Heat (Vol. 11)
Deadline (Vol. 12)
The Sword and the Iron Curtain (Vol. 13)

Sci-Fi

Zak Blue and the Great Space Chase Series:
Falcon Wing (Vol. 1)
Enter the Maelstrom (Vol. 2)

www.ingramcontent.com/pod-product-compliance
Lightning Source LLC
Chambersburg PA
CBHW072001040426
42447CB00009B/1426